PRESCRIPTION DRUG ABUSE AND DEPENDENCE:
How Prescription Drug Abuse Contributes to the Drug Abuse Epidemic

Publication Number 1088
AMERICAN SERIES IN BEHAVIORAL SCIENCE AND LAW

Edited by
RALPH SLOVENKO, B.E., LL.B., M.A., Ph.D.
Professor of Law and Psychiatry
Wayne State University
Law School
Detroit, Michigan

PRESCRIPTION DRUG ABUSE AND DEPENDENCE:
How Prescription Drug Abuse Contributes to the Drug Abuse Epidemic

By

DANIEL P. GREENFIELD, M.D., M.P.H., M.S.

Diplomate in Psychiatry and Addiction Medicine
Managing Partner
Brown and Greenfield Physician Consultants
Short Hills, New Jersey

and

Clinical Assistant Professor
Department of Psychiatry
Montefiore Medical Center/
Albert Einstein College of Medicine
Bronx, New York

With a Foreword by

Richard J. Russo, M.S.P.H.
Former Deputy Commissioner of Health
(Narcotics and Drug Abuse Control)
State of New Jersey

C H A R L E S   C   T H O M A S • P U B L I S H E R
Springfield • Illinois • U.S.A.

Published and Distributed Throughout the World by

CHARLES C THOMAS • PUBLISHER
2600 South First Street
Springfield, Illinois 62794-9265

© *1995 by* CHARLES C THOMAS • PUBLISHER
ISBN 0-398-05931-4
Library of Congress Catalog Card Number: 94-30116

Printed in the United States of America
SC-R-3

Library of Congress Cataloging-in-Publication Data

Greenfield, Daniel P.
   Prescription drug abuse and dependence : how prescription drug
abuse contributes to the drug abuse epidemic / by Daniel P.
Greenfield ; with a foreword by Richard J. Russo.
      p.   cm.
   Includes bibliographical references and index.
   ISBN 0-398-05931-4
   1. Medication abuse.   I. Title.
RM146.5.G74   1994
362.29 — dc20
                                                                94-30116
                                                                CIP

CONTRIBUTORS

JEFFREY A. BROWN, M.D., J.D., M.P.H., Managing Partner, Brown and Greenfield Physician Consultants (Short Hills, New Jersey), and Clinical Assistant Professor of Psychiatry, U.M.D.N.J.—New Jersey Medical School, Newark, New Jersey

EDWARD J. FLYNN, PH.D., Director of the Institute for Scientific and Chemical Literacy in New Jersey, and Associate Professor of Pharmacology and Toxicology, U.M.D.N.J.—New Jersey Medical School, Newark, New Jersey

ED FRANKLIN, JR., therapist, Scott and White Alcohol and Drug Dependence Treatment Program, Temple, Texas

DANIEL P. GREENFIELD, M.D., M.P.H., M.S., Managing Partner, Brown and Greenfield Physician Consultants (Short Hills, New Jersey), and Clinical Assistant Professor of Psychiatry, Montefiore Medical Center/Albert Einstein College of Medicine, Yeshiva University, Bronx, New York

PAMELA E. HALL, PSY.D., private practice of psychology (Summit, New Jersey), and Adjunct Associate Professor of Psychology, Pace University, New York, New York

JEFFREY S. KAHN, PH.D., private practice of psychology and addictive disorders, in Summit, New Jersey

RAYMOND KRYCH, PH.D., Program Director, Scott and White Alcohol and Drug Dependence Treatment Program, Temple, Texas, and Associate Professor in Psychiatry and Behavioral Sciences, Texas A & M University

RICHARD J. RUSSO, M.S.P.H., former Deputy Commissioner of Health (Narcotics and Dangerous Drugs), State of New Jersey

DAVID A. SCHWARTZ, J.D., private practice of criminal law, San Francisco, California, and former Public Defender in New Jersey and Pennsylvania

PHILIP H. WITT, PH.D., partner, Associates in Psychological Services (Somerville, New Jersey), and Clinical Assistant Professor in Psychiatry, U.M.D.N.J.—Robert Wood Johnson Medical School, Piscataway, New Jersey

To my parents, Dorothy and Leonard; my wife, Marguerite; my children, Jeremy, Sarah, and Katherine; my brother, Donald; my co-authors and colleagues who made this volume possible; and my office staff, especially Nicholle, who made the manuscript possible.

FOREWORD

PRESCRIPTION DRUG ABUSE:
THE "SILENT DEPENDENCY"

Controlled dangerous substances such as the psychotropics, C.N.S. stimulants, C.N.S. depressants, and the analgesics possess a desired therapeutic response and an addiction forming liability, and as such they present a dual pharmacological action which can be both life saving and life threatening. This unique characteristic to be both "good" and "bad" (with a thin line of separation between) is unique to this class of ethically manufactured prescription drugs and all of us who use these drugs have the potential for becoming dependent on them. The cavalier prescribing practices or the lack of sensitivity to the potential dependency syndrome by some practitioners permits and sometimes encourages over use and dependence of these specialty products. All of us, the prescriber, the dispenser, and the patient must become more aware and sensitized to the potential danger of these specialty drug products, because these drugs can foster a "silent dependency" which may take years to reverse in some, and may be irreversible in others.

The biblical phrase, "There but for the grace of God go I" applies to all of us who use these drugs.

RICHARD J. RUSSO, M.S.P.H.

ix

PREFACE

It has been said that the ultimate goal of medical care is for physicians and other providers of that care to be in the business to put themselves out of business.

However, physicians, other providers, and patients, do not always cooperate.

In fact, a particularly difficult area of patient lack of cooperation, or noncompliance, is in the area of prescription drug abuse and dependence (PDAD). PDAD is defined as "medicinals manufactured by the pharmaceutical industry . . . used in ways . . . not intended by regulatory agencies and . . . not approved by the mainstream culture."* Although not an extensive contributor to the substance abuse epidemic in this country, PDAD is nevertheless a significant cause of anxiety, frustration, and—of course—morbidity and mortality for prescribers and users alike in this troubling area of "licit" drug abuse.

In this monograph, the authors discuss PDAD from a variety of perspectives, in three broad sections. In the first section ("Overview of Prescription Drug Abuse and Dependence"), the authors review the nature, scope, and extent (epidemiologic) of PDAD, including chapters on the psychopharmacologic basis of PDAD, a classification of PDAD users, and the current status of benziodiazepine prescribing.

In the second section ("Assessment and Diagnosis") of the monograph the authors discuss practical aspects of interviewing and evaluating PDAD patients, psychological assessment of PDAD patients, and considerations about "dual diagnosis" patients (i.e., patients with substance abuse disorders and primary psychiatric disorders). In this section, as in the following section, the authors make the important point that practically speaking, the only significant difference between prescription drug abusers ("licit" drug abusers) and "street" drug abusers ("illicit" drug

---

*Wesson, D. & Smith, D. (1990). Prescription drug abuse. Patient, physician and cultural responsibilities. *Western Journal of Medicine, 152:* 613–616.

abusers) is the source of the drugs abused: The drugs themselves, their pharmacologic classes and properties, and the other clinical issues and considerations pertaining to abuse of these drugs are the same in both types of drug abusers, regardless of the source of the drugs.

In the last section of the monograph ("Clinical and Legal Interventions"), the authors discuss clinical treatment methods and legal issues and dispositions pertaining to PDAD, reviewing material relevant both to prescribers and users.

The ways in which PDAD can be deleterious to medical care, the doctor-patient relationship, and society in general can be far-reaching, extensive, and traumatic to doctors and patients alike. In the experience of the authors, PDAD tends to be underestimated and underplayed in professional training, continuing education, and practice. By reviewing this topic and presenting material from a practical, biopsychosocial, and broad perspective, the authors of this monograph have addressed an important aspect of health care—an aspect which is more often an impediment to good health care than health care providers might be aware of or than they would want to acknowledge.

RALPH SLOVENKO
Editor, American Series in
Behavioral Science and Law

CONTENTS

SECTION III
CONCLUSION

PRESCRIPTION DRUG ABUSE AND DEPENDENCE:
How Prescription Drug Abuse Contributes to the Drug Abuse Epidemic

Chapter 1

PRESCRIPTION DRUG ABUSE AND DEPENDENCE: AN INTRODUCTION

Daniel P. Greenfield

In this monograph, we will address a variety of facets of a small but significant contribution to substance abuse, namely prescription drug abuse and dependence (PDAD). By that term, we mean the *abuse* of prescribed medications, by patients, the excessive *use* of. prescribed medication, or the illegal or inappropriate obtaining of prescription medications through the diversion of prescribed medications from physicians, pharmacies, pharmaceutical manufacturing facilities and so forth. Wesson and Smith (1990) describe PDAD as follows: "Prescription drug abuse is a nebulous construct whose common denominator is that medicinals manufactured by the pharmaceutical industry are being used in ways that were not intended by regulatory agencies and in ways that are not approved by the mainstream culture . . . [this includes] . . . a range of patient, physician, and addict behavior . . . " (Wesson and Smith, 1990). Although recent data suggest that the prevalence of this problem may be declining (DAWN Reports, 1988–1991), studies also indicate that about 3 percent of " . . . patients . . . misuse such medications or take psychoactive drugs for the purpose of intoxication . . . " (Wilford, 1990), and National Institute of Drug Abuse (NIDA) surveys indicate that more than half of patients who sought treatment for or died of drug-related medical problems were abusing prescription drugs (Wilford, 1987). Regardless of the actual statistics or prevalence, the PDAD problem is a real one, and clearly presents distressing situations on the level of public health considerations as well as on the level of the individual clinician and patient.

A CLINICAL EPIDEMIOLOGY APPROACH

Using the model of the "epidemiologic triangle" (Mausner and Kramer, 1985) of "host," "agent," and "environment" as a paradigm for PDAD, the "host" in this model can be considered the physician (or pharmacy, or pharmaceutical manufacturing facility; for purposes of this chapter, we will consider only the physician) from whose practice prescription medications are diverted; the "agent" can be considered the medication (usually psychoactive and a "Controlled Dangerous Substance," or "CDS" (Comprehensive Drug Abuse Control and Prevention Act, 1970) diverted from the physician's practice; and the "environment" can be considered a combination of patients (who for a variety of reasons divert medications from prescriber's practices) and the overall sociocultural environment of substance abuse (as the context in which PDAD take place). We will discuss each of these three aspects of PDAD in turn.

The Host

Approximately one third of all disciplinary actions taken in 1990 by state boards of healing arts against those licensees able to prescribe medications were related to prescribing practices of abusable drugs and/or CDS (Voth, Dupont, and Voth, 1991). For a number of years, the American Medical Association (AMA) has recognized the gravity and magnitude of this problem, and has organized continuing and ongoing educational efforts over the years (meetings, publications, and others) to address this problem (Smith and Seymore, 1980). The Council of Scientific Affairs of the AMA in its report entitled "Drug Abuse Related to Prescribing Practices" (Council Report, 1982) identified a number of factors involved in PDAD applicable to the prescribing health-care provider. That report characterized four types (the "four D's") of physicians, specifically, involved as "hosts" (in the epidemiologic triangle model) in PDAD as described in Table 1-1.

In our experience, the "host" prescribers in this epidemiologic triangle model most difficult to work with are the "duped" and "dated" doctors. Fortunately, these prescribers also tend to be amenable toward the educational programs available for them. In addition, the "disabled" (impaired) prescribers are benefited by a proliferating number of rehabilitation programs and facilities available to them, in recognition of the problem of the impaired professional (Canavan, 1983).

**Table 1-1. The Four D's in Prescription Drug Abuse and Dependence
(Adapted from Council Report, 1982)**

(1) "The willful and conscious misprescribing of controlled substances for drug abuse purposes, and usually for profit. These are the "script doctors" . . . who should be prosecuted to the full extent of the law."

(2) "Inappropriate prescribing by physicians who unwittingly acquiesce to persistent demands by patients for medication. These are the "duped doctors." Typically, in these cases, drugs are prescribed in excessive amount or for longer periods than necessary. The result can be the initiation or perpetuation of drug abuse or drug dependence in the patient or diversion of the drug to other persons for abuse purposes."

(3) "Uninformed prescribing by physicians who have not kept abreast of new developments in pharmacology and drug therapy. These are the "dated doctors." In addition to prescribing excessive amounts of drugs or for excessive amounts of time, drugs can be prescribed for conditions that do not warrant chemotherapy or that might better be treated by other drugs."

(4) "Self-prescribing and administration by physicians who themselves are drug abusers or are drug dependent. These are "impaired (or "disabled" Ed.) doctors" who are in need of treatment and who may have to have their licenses to practice restricted or suspended. Rehabilitation and disciplinary programs already exist in most states through medical societies and boards of medical examiners."

These types are known as "Dishonest," "Duped," "Dated," and "Disabled" (the "four D's"), respectively; in the case of types (1) and (2), patients contribute significantly to PDAD.

The Agent

In a previous publication on the topic of PDAD, Weiss and Greenfield (1986) outlined four broad categories of PDAD drugs, of PDAD, including psychoactive drugs and agents (the largest group of PDAD drugs) and a heterogeneous group which they called "unexpected" PDAD agents. The first three categories consist of *stimulants* (such as amphetamines, methylphenidate [Ritalin], and anorexiants ["diet pills"]); *depressants* (opioids, narcotics, benzodiazepines, barbiturates, and nonbarbiturate hypnotics); and *hallucinogens* (volatile inhalants, phencyclidine [PCP] and congeners, L.S.D., and others. Since prescription of these agents is rarely permitted under federal and state law, they do not represent a major portion of PDAD). The fourth, and last category ("unexpected" agents) consists of such diverse compounds as beta-blockers (Lehrer, Rosen, Kostis, and Greenfield, 1987); "transitional" drugs (such as analgesics and antitussives) which may lead to excessive licit or illicit drug use (Carloss, 1979; Chasnoff, Diggs, and Schnoll, 1981); antibiotics (Chretien, McGarvey, deStwolinski, et al., 1975); and over the counter (OTC) preparations (especially cough and sleep preparations with anticholinergic effects and home remedies for colds, with decongestant and antihistamine properties and side effects) (Ray, 1983; Vener, Krupka, and Cline, 1982). These broad categories of drugs of PDAD emphasize two important practical aspects in our experience about PDAD, namely (1) it would be impossible, as a practical clinical matter, to separate PDAD from other types of substance abuse since both types of abuse frequently coexist and since the properties and types of drugs abused are the same, whether they are illegally obtained "from the street" ("illicit drug abuse") or legally—at least initially—through a prescription ("licit drug abuse"); and (2) the drug abusers themselves are essentially the same in many respects, again whether they obtain their drugs "licitly" (through prescription diversion) or "illicitly" ("from the street").

In the context of the "agent" in the PDAD epidemiologic triangle model, it is important to note that the majority of drugs diverted from prescribers are (so-called) "Controlled Dangerous Substances," or "CDS," (Comprehensive Drug Abuse Control and Prevention Act, 1970), the prescribing of which is regulated by state and federal law. While a detailed review of the CDS law and its various schedules of CDS drugs is beyond the scope of this chapter, we have listed some representative drugs under the five Federal Schedules of the CDS law (Table 1-2), and have also listed in Table 3, the bases for assignment and prescribing requirements for CDS (Wilford, 1981).

The Environment

Finally, the third part in the epidemiologic triangle model for PDAD—the "environment"—can be considered to be a combination of patients, or clients who for a variety of reasons divert medications from prescribers' practices and of the overall sociocultural environment of substance abuse where the PDAD takes place. The client/patients are protean in their appearance, presenting a wide range of psychopathology (Kornblith, 1981), a variety of physical signs and symptoms (e.g., pain syndromes, insomnia, anxiety, depression, and obesity [Weiss and Greenfield, 1986]), and in some instances, a prior history of planned or inadvertent substance abuse or PDAD, especially among the elderly (Glantz, 1981).

Table 1-2. Controlled Prescription Drugs, Federal Schedules.

Class of Drug	Schedule I	Schedule II	Schedule III	Schedule IV	Schedule V
Hallucinogens	Marijuana LSD	—	—	—	—
Stimulants	Congeners of amphetamines	Amphetamine Methamphetamine	Mazindol Phendimetrazine Other anorexiants	Diethylpropion Phentermine	—
Narcotic analgesics	Heroin	Codeine	Combination such as APC + codeine, ASA + codeine		
	1-alpha acetyl methadol (LAAM)	Methadone Oxycodone Morphine			
Depressants		Amobarbital Secobarbital	Glutethimide Unscheduled drug + amobarbital, and so forth	All benzodiazepines	
				Mixtures containing small quantities of narcotics, generally for antitussive and antidiarrheal purposes. Available under some circumstances without prescription.	

A number of diagnostic and classification schemes to describe substance abusers has been proposed by various groups and organizations over the years. We endorse the system used in the *Diagnostic and Statistical Manual of Mental Disorders, Fourth Edition (DSM-IV)* (1994) of the American Psychiatric Association, for several reasons: (1) The multiaxial diagnostic system of the *DSM-IV* presents a broader practical clinical picture of an individual with a psychiatric disorder (including substance abuse and/or dependence) than do other schemes with which we are familiar; (2) The dual classification system of substance abusers in the *DSM-IV* emphasizes both the *consequences* of substance abuse (called "Psychoactive Substance Induced Organic Mental Disorders"—i.e., organic brain damage) and the *behaviors* (drug seeking behaviors) of the substance abuser (called "Psychoactive Substance Abuse" and "Psychoactive Substance Depen-

**Table 1-3. Bases for Assignment and Prescribing Requirements
for Controlled Prescription Drugs.**

Schedule	Basis for Assignment	Prescribing Requirements
I	The drug or other substance has (1) a high potential for abuse; (2) no accepted medical use in U.S.; and (3) a lack of accepted safety for medical use	Not prescribable by private physicians
II	The drug or other substance has (1) a high potential for abuse; (2) an accepted medical use; and (3) potential for severe psychological or physical dependence	Prescriptions must be signed and given adequate identifying patient information; must bear the federal DEA (and state equivalent) registration number of the prescriber; must be limited in quantity to a 30-day or 120-dose supply (whichever is less); may not be telephoned, except in very unusual circumstances
III	The drug or other substance has (1) a potential for abuse less than Schedule I or II substances; (2) an accepted medical use; and (3) potential for moderate or low physical or psychological dependence	Prescriptions must be signed and given adequate identifying patient information; must bear prescriber's DEA number; may be refilled five times or for a 6-month period (whichever comes first); may be telephoned; no limit on quantity
IV	The drug or other substance has (1) a potential for abuse less than Schedule III substances; (2) an accepted medical use; and (3) limited potential for physical or psychological dependence	Same as for Schedule III
V	The drug or other substance has (1) a potential for abuse less than Schedule IV substances; (2) an accepted medical use; and (3) potential for dependence less than other four Schedules	Same as for Schedules III and IV except they (1) may be refilled for up to one year and (2) are available without prescription under certain circumstances

dence") as well as interactions between these two features of the abuser; (3) The diagnostic criteria for *behaviors* associated with substance abuse, in our opinion, represent a realistic clinical approach to understanding and working with the substance abuser (e.g., *DSM-IV* diagnostic criteria for "Psychoactive Substance Abuse" include: [1] continued use despite knowledge of having a persistent or recurrent social, occupational, psychological, or physical problem that is caused or exacerbated by use of the psychoactive substance, "[or]" [2] recurrent use in situations in which use is physically hazardous (e.g. "driving while intoxicated"); and (4) The multiaxial diagnostic system of the *DSM-IV* permits useful clinical characterization of individuals with both primary psychiatric disorders and substance abuse disorders (i.e., individuals with so-called "dual diagnosis," or "mentally ill chemical abuser" disorders, which are increasingly prevalent types of client/patients whose needs include treatment for both their psychiatric and substance abuse disorders (Reilly, 1991). Briefly, the multiaxial classification system of the *DSM-IV* is described in Table 1-4, and the major categories of "Psychoactive Substance-Induced Organic Mental Disorders" and "Psychoactive Substance Abuse/Dependence" Disorders are presented in Table 1-5 and Table 1-6, respectively.

Table 1-4. Multiaxial Diagnostic System
(*after DSM-IV, 1994*).

Axis I	Clinical Disorders
	Other Conditions That May Be a Focus of Clinical Attention
Axis II	Personality Disorders
	Mental Retardation
Axis III	General Medical Conditions
Axis IV	Psychological and Environmental Problems
Axis V	Global Assessment of Functioning

With regard to the overall socio-cultural environment of substance abuse in which PDAD takes place, we have already made the point that practically speaking, it is impossible to separate PDAD from other types of substance abuse. Both types frequently coexist, because accurate epidemiologic data teasing out the contributions both types make to substance abuse are not available, and, again, the only real difference between the "licit" and "illicit" drug abuser is how the abuser obtains his/her drugs—not in any differential response on the abuser's part to the same drug.

Table 1-5. Substance-Related Disorders:
Substance-Induced Disorders
(after DSM–IV, 1994).

- Alcohol
- Amphetamine or amphetamine-like sympathomimetic
- Caffeine
- Cannabis
- Cocaine
- Hallucinogen
- Inhalant
- Nicotine
- Opioid
- Phencyclidine (PCP) or phencyclidine-like
- Sedative, hypnotic, or anxiolytic
- Other (or unknown) substance

Table 1-6. Substance-Related Disorder:
Substance Use Disorders
(after DSM–IV, 1994).

- Alcohol
- Amphetamine or amphetamine-like sympathomimetic
- Cannabis
- Cocaine
- Hallucinogen
- Inhalant
- Nicotine
- Opioid
- Phencyclidine (PCP) or phencyclidine-like
- Sedative, hypnotic, or anxiolytic
- Polysubstance

THIS MONOGRAPH

We have produced this monograph to respond to real and perceived problems and public concerns associated with PDAD, and we have structured this monograph in keeping with points raised earlier in this chapter. The first section of the monograph presents "An Overview of Prescription Drug Abuse and Dependence."

In Chapter 2 ("Psychoactive Drugs and Their Effects"), Edward Flynn reviews the main categories of psychoactive drugs, and discusses their pharmacologic and behavioral effects on users of these drugs. This chapter provides a foundation for the rest of the monograph in terms of topics dealing with the "agent" (in the epidemiologic triangle of model of PDAD).

Raymond Krych, Philip Witt, and Ed Franklin, Jr. next (Chapter 3) present "A Taxonomy of Prescription Drug Abuse and Dependency." The authors describe from a psychological and motivational perspective a series of types of prescription drug users. Their taxonomy, in our opinion, goes beyond the phenomenologically-oriented *DMS-IV* diagnostic criteria and categories, and provides an interesting and thought-provoking approach to evaluating and treating prescription drug users, a part of the "environment" in the epidemiologic triangle model of PDAD.

Any contemporary discussion of PDAD would be incomplete without addressing the current status of the benzodiazepines, still among the most prescribed and controversial drugs in the world (Applebaum, 1982). Chapter 4, entitled "Current Status in Medicolegal Aspects of Presenting Benzodiazepines: A Special Case," by Daniel Greenfield and Jeffrey Brown, reviews clinical/medical and legal aspects of this frequently prescribed class of Controlled Dangerous Substances (CDS). In this chapter, the authors emphasize therapeutic and nontherapeutic uses of benzodiazepines, describe medicolegal aspects of judicious prescribing of these drugs, and review regulatory approaches to the control of benzodiazepine prescribing.

Moving from the section of this monograph dealing with "An Overview of Prescription Drug Abuse and Dependence" to the section addressing "Assessment and Diagnosis," Greenfield and Brown in Chapter 5 ("Interviewing the Difficult Patient") discuss the commonly-encountered clinical problem of interviewing difficult and uncooperative client/patients who may have an ulterior motive or hidden agenda for seeking professional "help." The authors use the case example of a PDAD client/patient as a basis for their discussion, and they offer some practical suggestions and strategies in working with such clients/patients.

In Chapter 6 ("Psychological Assessment of the Prescription Drug Abuser: Clinical and Testing"), Pamela Hall reviews a diagnostic and evaluation approach and system for assessing PDAD clients/patients, or for that matter, any drug abusers or chemically dependent persons. Hall describes interviewing and psychological test and inventory techniques, offering a comprehensive and generic approach to this assessment, recognizing—as is done periodically throughout this monograph—that PDAD clients/patients and other types of drug abusing/dependent clients/patients differ from one another significantly only in the ways in which they obtain their drugs (i.e., "licitly," or "illicitly," as described above), and that there is often overlap between these two ways.

Continuing the presentation of clinical material, Jeffrey Kahn discusses "Diagnostic Entities: Anxiety, Panic, and Mood Disorders and Cases" in Chapter 7. Kahn reviews the *DSM-IV* classification of individuals with these types of psychiatric disorders, discusses interactions and dynamics between these disorders and clients/patients who constantly use/abuse psychoactive substances (another example of "dual diagnoses" clients/ patients), and presents and discusses case material involving PDAD and other drug abuse and dependent clients/patients.

Concluding the monograph with a section entitled "Clinical and Legal Interventions," the first chapter of this section (Chapter 9: "An Overview of Treatment Modalities" by Pamela Hall and Daniel Greenfield) reviews the range of treatment opportunities available to PDAD clients/patients and other drug abuse/dependent clients/patients. Although Hall and Greenfield point out the similarities between PDAD clients/patients and other drug abuse/dependent individuals, they also describe one area of treatment unique to prescribers, namely programs and facilities for "impaired professionals" (Canavan, 1983).

As with the benzodiazepines (Chapter 4), a contemporary discussion of PDAD would be incomplete without addressing legal aspects, constraints, and consequences of PDAD. David Schwartz and Daniel Greenfield address these several aspects in Chapter 9 ("Legal Dispositions and Interventions"), describing duties and responsibilities of health-care providers (prescribers) and clients/patients with respect to PDAD; reviewing civil and criminal offenses and remedies regarding PDAD; and providing guidelines for safe, efficacious, and judicious prescribing practices.

At the end of this monograph, entitled "In Conclusion: An Epilogue," the editor, Daniel Greenfield, reviews the salient features of the monograph, providing conclusions and advisory comments about the extent of PDAD, the responsibilities of "providers" and "consumers" (of prescription drugs), and suggestions about future research and intervention. He emphasizes that although PDAD constitutes a relatively small part of the total contemporary substance abuse picture, it is nevertheless a statistically and clinically significant part of that picture, and it therefore behooves clinicians and clients/patients alike to be aware of the problem, and to "do their part" in dealing with the problem.

REFERENCES

Applebaum, P. (1982). Controlling prescription of benzodiazepines. *Hospital and Community Psychiatry, 43:*12–13.

Carloss, A. (1979). Misuse of a "harmless" drug. *Archives of Internal Medicine, 139:*688–689.

Canavan, D. (1983). The subject of impairment. *Journal of the Medical Society of New Jersey, 80:*47–48.

Chasnoff, I. Diggs, G. and Schnoll, S. (1981). Fetal alcohol effects and maternal cough syrup abuse. *American Journal of Diseases of Children, 135:*968–970.

Chretien, J. McGarvey, M. deStwolinski, A. *et al.* (1975). Abuse of antibiotics: A study of patients attending a university clinic. *Archives of Internal Medicine, 135:*1063–1065.

Comprehensive Drug Abuse Prevention and Control Act of 1970 (1970) 21 *U.S.C.* 812(6) 2(c).

Council Report (Council on Scientific Affairs, American Medical Association) (1982). Drug abuse related to prescribing practices. *Journal of the American Medical Association, 247:*864–866.

Drug Abuse Warning Network (1988–1991). *Statistical Series, Series 1, Numbers 8, 9, 10, 11.* Washington, D.C., U.S.D.H.H.S. (National Institute on Drug Abuse).

Glantz, M. (1981). Predictors of elderly drug abuse. *Journal of Psychoactive Drugs, 13:*117–126.

Kornblith, A. (1981). Multiple drug abuse involving nonopiate, nonalcoholic substances. I. Prevalence. *International Journal of the Addictions, 16:*197–232.

Lehrer, P. Rosen, R. Kostis, J. and Greenfield, D. (1987). Treating stage fright in musicians: The use of beta blockers. *Journal of the Medical Society of New Jersey, 84:*27–33.

Mausner, J. and Kramer, S. (1985). *Mausner and Bahn, Epidemiology—An Introductory Text.* Philadelphia: W. B. Saunders.

Multiple authors (1987). *Diagnostic and Statistical Manual of Mental Disorders, Third Edition, Revised,* Washington, D. C.: American Psychiatric Association.

Ray, O. (1983). *Drugs, Society, and Human Behavior (Third Edition)* St. Louis: C. V. Mosby.

Reilly, P. (1991). Assessment and treatment of the mentally ill chemical abuser and the family. *Journal of Chemical Dependency Treatment, 4:*167–178.

Smith, D. and Seymore, R. (1980). Prescribing practices: The educational alternative for the misprescriber. Proceedings of the White House Conference on Prescription Drug Abuse, Washington, D.C. U.S.D.H.H.S. (N.I.D.A.).

Vener, A. Krupka, L. and Cline, J. (1982). Drugs (prescription, over-the-counter, social) and the young adult: Use and attitudes. *International Journal of the Addictions,* *17:*399–415.

Voth, E. Dupont, R. and Voth, H. (1991). Responsible prescribing of controlled substances, *American Family Physician, 44:*1673–1678.

Weiss, K. and Greenfield, D. (1986). Prescription drug abuse. *Psychiatric Clinics of North America, 9:*475–490.

Wesson, D. and Smith, D. (1990). Prescription drug abuse. Patient, physician and cultural responsibilities. *Western Journal of Medicine, 152:*613–616.

Wilford, B. (1990). Abuse of prescription drugs. *Western Journal of Medicines, 152:*609–612.

Wilford, B. (1981). *Drug Abuse. A Guide for the Primary Care Physician.* Chicago: American Medical Association.

Wilford, B. (1987). *Prescribing Controlled Drugs.* Chicago: American Medical Association.

Chapter 2

PSYCHOTROPIC DRUGS AND THEIR EFFECTS

Edward J. Flynn

BACKGROUND

There has been consistent concern over the abuse of both licit and illicit drugs that is reflected in the passage of numerous laws and regulations beginning in 1906 and continuing as in the recently enacted designer drug laws (Congressional Record, 1906; Lawrence, 1988). The number of patients involved in prescription drug abuse may be as large as 3 percent of the population. Surveys by the National Institute on Drug Abuse on the consequences of such use found that more than half of patients who sought treatment for or died of drug-related medical problems were abusing prescription drugs (NHSDA, 1990). Furthermore, the Council on Scientific Affairs of the American Medical Association described the problem of physicians contributing to prescription drug abuse and made suggestions for steps to be taken to deal with this health problem (Hughes et al., 1992). Prescription drug abuse involves medicinal preparations made by the pharmaceutical industry being used in ways that are counter to established medical practices. Most often this is reflected as a tendency to increase the dose beyond necessary or recommended levels, to use the drug more frequently than intended or to use the drug for inappropriately extended periods of time (American Psychiatric Association, 1987).

Many psychotropic (*psycho,* mind, spirit, soul, mental processes; *tropic,* turning, changing, acting upon) drugs and drug classes can be subject to prescription drug abuse and street drug abuse. Among the major drug types that can lead to dependence and/or drug abuse are the opioids, stimulants, and depressants (sedative-hypnotics and antianxiety drugs) (Brady and Lukas, 1984; Kalant and Kalant, 1971; Griffiths et al., 1979). There is also concern with some drug groups that share properties with the major psychotropic drugs. In this category would be a variety of antihistamines (allergy and cold preparations), antitussives (cough

15

suppressants), and even some drugs used to control blood pressure (beta blockers) (Ray and Ksir, 1990; Matthys et al., 1983; Gengo et al., 1987). In addition, it is known that patients and medical personnel represent risk groups for developing dependence/abuse on psychotropic medications because of dispositional factors and availability of these drugs (McAuliffe et al., 1986; Murray, 1978).

ACUTE AND CHRONIC DRUG–TAKING COMPARISONS

Prior to describing the effects of the major groups of psychotropic drugs, it is important to mention that the symptoms that are seen following a given drug are often related to the length of time an individual is "on the drug." In acute drug administration, it is the events surrounding the sudden onset, sharp rise and short duration following a single dose that are important to assess. The result of taking many single doses over months or years is of concern when chronic drug exposure is described. An emphasis is placed on a description of drug effects that includes consideration of acute and chronic drug exposure, since each pattern of drug usage has its distinct set of health problems.

Acute drug-taking behavior leads to health concerns generally related to overdosage, drug-drug interactions or accidents while under the influence of the drug. Dose-response curves are included to show the multiple effects that occur as dosage shifts from therapeutic range to toxic levels. The important problems that arise from addition or synergism when drugs are taken in combination are not considered. Psychotropic drugs, as part of their allure, produce a lessening of social inhibitions and therefore the chance of "unsafe" behavior increases. Numerous examples exist among street drug abusers of people injuring themselves during activities unlikely to occur while sober. These incidents along with well-documented toxicities arising from high doses and widely appreciated drug combinations are particular problems during acute drug exposure (Cregler, 1989: Martin, 1983). The signs and symptoms occurring during acute drug exposure are quite predictable based on current understanding of the mechanism of action of the particular psychotropic drug (Gilman et al., 1990).

On the other hand, during chronic drug exposure, symptoms often arise from physiological malfunctions that have little relationship to the psychotropic activity leading to dependence and abuse. For example, there is no obvious relationship between ethanol's ability to depress nervous tissue causing intoxication and its production of liver disease following long-term exposure. Similarly, there is no clear correlation between sensitivity to cocaine's euphorogenic effects and the sensitivity of the cardiovascular system to its effects (Karch, 1988). The sections that follow describe some of the major organ systems of the body that may begin to develop symptoms as an individual engages in chronic drug taking. However, it is important to remember that many of the central problems of chronic drug intake are the consequences of the psychotropic effect itself. Even though tolerance to the "mind altering" effect is the rule, the individual involved in chronic drug exposure is continually interacting with his or her environment (persons, places and things) utilizing an altered perceptual system. Years of such drug taking can lead to numerous misperceptions and misconceptions. One consequence of this behavior is the denial process, wherein all aspects of an individual (physical, mental, social, spiritual, emotional) are crumbling due to drug use which is obvious to family and friends, but are seemingly unrelated to drug use in the opinion of the abuser.

Table 2-1. Comparison of Acute vs Chronic Health Problems
for Cocaine Exposure.

Exposure Duration	Psychotropic Effects	Other Physiologic Effects
Acute	Decreased Fatigue	Increased Heart Rate
	Anorexia	Increased Blood Pressure
	Enhanced Sexuality	Increased Temperature
	Euphoria	
Chronic	Fatigue	Hypertension
	Weight Loss	Congestive Heart Failure
	Impotence	Pulmonary Disease
	Dysphoria	Muscular Twitching

To illustrate the difference between acute and chronic drug symptoms, these symptoms are compared for the drug cocaine. Table 2-1 illustrates the acute and chronic psychotropic and other physiologic effects for the stimulant drug, cocaine. As can be seen in the table, the effects seen acutely may be quite the opposite of those found when drug administration becomes chronic. In addition, some physiologic systems that are transiently influenced during an acute exposure progress into chronic diseases. These conditions are serious health problems and often require therapy along with treatment of the primary diagnosis of drug dependence/abuse.

EFFECTS OF PSYCHOTROPIC DRUGS

The discussion below describes some of the predictable pharmacologic actions following acute and chronic drug administration of common psychotropic drugs both to the central nervous system (brain and spinal cord) and other major organ systems (heart, lung, kidney, gastrointestinal tract, liver) (Gilman et al., 1990).

Opioids

Opioids refer to a group of drugs that are opium or morphine-like in pharmacologic characteristics (Gilman et al., 1990). The opioids are a major category of drugs that are subject to prescription and street abuse. Historically, these drugs were called narcotics or opiates, but the term opioid is now preferred. Table 2-2 lists some of the common examples of opioids currently available.

Table 2-2. Representative Examples of Opioid Drugs

Nonproprietary Name	Trade Name
Morphine	
Heroin	
Hydromorphone	Dilaudid
Methadone	Dolophine
Meperidine	Demerol
Fentanyl	Sublimaze
Codeine	
Hydrocodone	Hycodan
Propoxyphene	Darvon
Buprenorphine	Buprenex
Pentazocine	Talwin
Nalbuphine	Nubain
Butorphanol	Stadol

Central Nervous System

The opioids are employed therapeutically, primarily as analgesics and antidiarrheal medications, but they have a variety of other pharmacological actions. In the body, opioids interact with several receptor types to produce effects similar to three families of endogenous neuropeptides (enkephalins, endorphins, and dynorphins) (Bloom, 1983; Akil et al., 1984; Goldstein, 1984).

Even though opioids are generally prescribed for pain relief, it is their ability to produce mood changes (euphoria, tranquility) that leads to significant abuse potential. The psychotropic effect becomes more prominent as the dose is increased, the route of administration is changed, or a more lipid soluble derivative is taken to more quickly increase the drug concentration in the brain. In addition to analgesia and altered mood, opioids invariably produce respiratory depression as a result of a direct action on brainstem respiratory centers. The respiratory depression occurs at doses below that effecting consciousness, but all phases of breathing decrease further as the dose is increased (Martin, 1983). Most opioids also cause constriction of pupils (miosis). In fact, the triad of unconsciousness, severe respiratory depression, and pinpoint pupils are characteristic of opioid overdose. Virtually all opioid overdose lethality results from respiratory depression. The acute administration of opioids produces the dose-related effects shown in Figure 2-1.

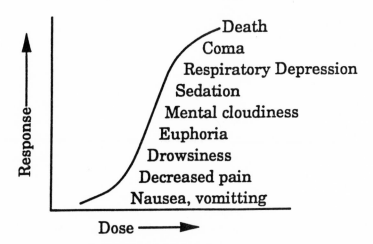

Figure 2-1. Theoretical Dose-Response Curves for Opioid Drugs.

When opioids are taken chronically, the dose response relationships shown in the figure are shifted to the right, so that while nearly identical effects can be produced, the dose required to elicit them is increased (tolerance) (Goudie and Demellweek, 1986). Although chronic exposure leads to tolerance to many of a drug's effects, it does not follow that tolerance occurs to all of a drug's effects. With opioids, tolerance is found to the euphorogenic effect, but not to the miotic or constipating actions. At the same time, drug dependence can develop. The degree of dependence that results is often due to a combination of the particular opioids' ability to produce reinforcing euphoria coupled with its ability to cause physical dependence and therefore, withdrawal symptoms sufficient to lead to drug-seeking behavior.

Other Organ Systems

Opioids produce a number of actions along the gastrointestinal (GI) tract from the stomach to the small intestine and finally the large intestine. These actions contribute to the constipating effect of opioids that finds use in the treatment of diarrhea, but frequently is a nagging side effect for both the licit and illicit opioid user.

The opioids decrease gastric motility thereby prolonging stomach emptying time. Constriction of the antral portion of the stomach and the first part of the duodenum can prolong passage of stomach contents into the remainder of the small intestine. Decreased propulsive contraction of the small intestines and delayed digestion of food combined with removal of water from the bowel contents greatly increases viscosity of feces. Concomitant depression of propulsion of fecal material through the large intestine, increased tone of the colon, and further time to remove water and desiccate fecal matter considerably add to the slowing of movement of material through the GI tract. Opioid-induced increase in anal sphincter tone and lessened response to the sensory stimulus for defecation add to the constellation of opioid actions that lead to constipation.

Although, the major effects of opioids are the result of actions on the CNS or GI tract, other symptoms may arise from actions on the biliary tract (epigastric distress, colic), ureter and urinary bladder (urinary retention), or uterus (prolongation of labor). In addition, although opioids do not have major actions on the cardiovascular system, certain conditions may predispose individuals to opioid-induced problems. For example, individuals with decreased blood volume (hypovolemia) given morphine may go into shock. Similarly, opioids must be used with caution in individuals with respiration problems such as emphysema or cor pulmonale.

Stimulants

Stimulant drugs (Table 2-3) are among the most widely used classes of drugs (Arnaud, 1987). The stimulant, caffeine, is probably the most frequently ingested drug worldwide. In addition to caffeine's presence in a variety of beverages, it is also an ingredient in a host of prescription and over-the-counter preparations. While the therapeutic indication for stimulants is somewhat limited, their social use and potential for abuse is extremely high (Silverstone, 1986; Klein et al., 1980; Fischman and Schuster, 1982). Historically, stimulants are agents that improve mental and physical performance when they are impaired because of fatigue.

Table 2-3. Representative Examples of Stimulant Drugs.

Nonproprietary Name	Trade Name
Amphetamine	Biphetamine
Cocaine	
Dextroamphetamine	Dexadrine
Methamphetamine	Desoxyn
Phendimetrazine	Plegine, Bontril
Methylphenidate	Ritalin
Diethylpropion	Tenuate, Tepanil
Phenylpropanolamine	Naldecon, Ornade
Mazindol	Mazanor, Sanorex
Benzphetamine	Didrex

Central Nervous System

Stimulants drugs are used therapeutically to produce nasal decongestion, vasoconstriction, bronchodilation, anorexia and psychostimulation. Their potential for abuse resides in the last effect which is subjectively felt as an elevation in mood and a sense of increased energy and alertness. These effects, as with all centrally active drugs, are to a degree dependent on the particular stimulant taken, its route of administration and a group of biopsychosocial factors related to the individual user. The dose-related CNS effects following acute administration of stimulant drugs are shown in Figure 2-2. As illustrated in the figure, the lower end of the dose-response curve is characterized by increased activation and arousal of the CNS. With numerous stimulants this may simply be displayed by insomnia, thus the importance of stimulant use assessment as part of routine history taking. Motor activity may also increase. Eventually as the dose of stimulant is raised mental confusion results from the arousal level being too high. Information processing systems become overloaded and discrimination ability is lost leading to confusion and delusions. Acute anxiety and marked agitation are felt. Convulsions eventually occur and death as a result of cardiopulmonary arrest may result (Isner et al., 1986).

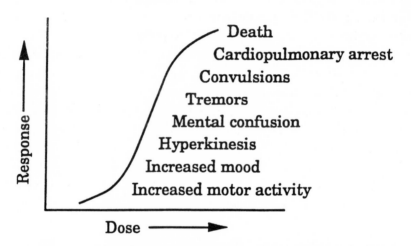

Figure 2-2. Theoretical Dose-Response Curves for Stimulant Drugs.

Along with the initial subjective euphoria, individuals display a decreased appetite and a reduced need for sleep. Both of these actions have been exploited in medicinal preparations for treatment of obesity and to delay the effects of fatigue (Klein et al., 1980). The increased energy and sociability that occur early on in stimulant use are often considered positive experiences and contribute to more frequent use of the drug and a tendency to increase the dose. Acute cocaine use may be associated with heightened sexual interest which coupled with impaired judgment and promiscuity contribute to transmission of venereal disease, including HIV infection.

Chronic stimulant drug abusers, particularly of cocaine or amphetamines, display delusions, suspiciousness, depression, irritability and dysphoria. In contrast to the acute effects of these drugs, chronic exposure is characterized more by an inability to concentrate, fatigue, and sexual disinterest or impotence. Sexual dysfunction is a common complaint among those seeking treatment (Siegel, 1984). Particularly with intravenous, high-dose, "binge" abusers of stimulants, a marked craving for the drug and visual and tactile hallucinations are seen. What initially is reality-based insight eventually gives way to anxiety, hypervigilance, and persecutory fears which may include aggressive or homicidal actions against imagined persecutions.

Other Organ Systems

Similar to the central nervous system effects described above, the mechanisms of action of stimulant agents predict the cardiovascular system should be a major target for stimulant side effects. They acutely increase heart rate and blood pressure. Common serious side effects include myocardial ischemia or infarction, myocarditis, cerebrovascular spasm, and intracerebral hemorrhage. Stimulants increase respiratory rate and cause dilated pupils. They may also increase body temperature. As the dose is increased toward toxic levels, hypertension worsens, tachycardia becomes more severe and irregular heart beats occur. Hyperthermia as high as 106–107 degrees F has been reported. Finally, cardiovascular collapse may lead to shock which, along with seizures and respiratory depression, may lead to death (Gawin and Ellinwood, 1988).

Depressants (Sedative/Hypnotics and Antianxiety Drugs)

This category includes a variety of drugs capable of producing a state of depression of the central nervous system resembling normal sleep. Some common examples of CNS depressants are listed in Table 2-4. Further classification is often based on clinical uses rather than similarity of chemical structure or mechanisms of action. The abuse potential of this group of drugs is often related to their physicochemical properties which control the rate at which they gain entrance into the CNS. Those drugs that enter most rapidly are subject to a higher incidence of abuse (Woods et al., 1987).

Central Nervous System

The dose-dependent depression of CNS function is shown in Figure 2-3 (Katzung, 1992). Two examples of such dose-response relationships are illustrated. The linear slope of line A is typical of older CNS

Table 2-4. Representative Examples of CNS Depressant Drugs.

Nonproprietary Name	Trade Name
Benzodiazepines	
Chlordiazepoxide	Librium, others
Clorazepate	Tranxene, others
Diazepam	Valium, others
Flurazepam	Dalmane, others
Lorazepam	Ativan, others
Oxazepam	Serax, others
Temazepam	Restoril, others
Triazolam	Halcion
Barbiturates	
Amobarbital	Amytal
Butabarbital	Butisol, others
Mephobarbital	Mebaral
Pentobarbital	Nembutal
Phenobarbital	Luminal, others
Secobarbital	Seconal
Miscellaneous	
Chloral hydrate	Noctec, others
Ethylchlorvinyl	Placidyl
Glutethimide	Doriden, others
Meprobamate	Miltown, others
Methyprylon	Noludar

depressants, such as barbiturates. These drugs are still employed therapeutically in symptomatic therapy of epilepsy and as intravenous anesthetics. However, the use of barbiturates has been greatly reduced by the availability of benzodiazepines whose effects are shown as line B. This figure depicts a major difference between these two groups of CNS depressants. In line A, it can be seen that as the dose is increased above that needed for hypnosis (sleep), a state of general anesthesia may occur. At still higher doses, such sedative-hypnotics may lead to depression of respiratory or vasomotor control in the brain leading to coma and death. In contrast, deviations from linearity, as shown in line B, require proportionately greater dosage increments in order to produce effects more profound than those required for hypnosis. It is this greater margin of safety of benzodiazepines that has led to their extensive use as antianxiety and hypnotic agents.

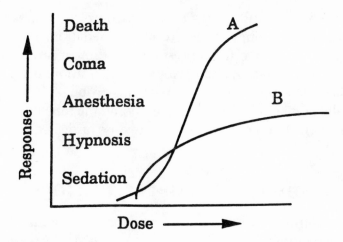

Figure 2-3. Theoretical Dose-Response Curves for CNS Depressants.

As a consequence of the ability to depress CNS function, these agents find therapeutic use as sedatives to moderate excitement and calm patients (anxiolytic activity). In hypnotic doses these drugs produce drowsiness and facilitate the onset and maintenance of sleep. The benzodiazepines, in addition, are employed as muscle relaxants, antiepileptic agents and to produce sedation and amnesia before and during surgery (Katzung, 1992).

As a result of their CNS depressing capability, agents of this type resemble the pharmacologic effect of ethanol and share its potential for abuse. At low doses these drugs can cause mild depression of the CNS without excessive drowsiness or inefficiency. As the dose in increased subjective feelings of relaxation, reduced social inhibitions, and increased sociability occur. The euphoric mood is difficult to maintain with ethanol and barbiturates since frequently the user slips into sedation. At such depressed levels of CNS arousal the individual may be neither aware of changes in their environment nor capable of responding to them. As the dose is increased, confusion, intellectual impairment, personality change, emotional liability, motor incoordination, staggering gait, slurred speech, and nystagmus occur. Higher doses, particularly with ethanol or the barbiturates, cause further CNS depression culminating in severe respiratory depression and death.

Other than ethanol, the sedative-hypnotic drugs do not have major effects on other organ systems. The major concerns are overdosage, their frequent interactions with other CNS depressants and the ability of some depressants to induce drug metabolizing enzymes.

Chronic administration leads to health concerns, generally a direct consequence of living in a state of continued sedation. The blunting of CNS function to perceive and process information for prolonged periods of time, coupled with frequent periods of intoxication, is considered an irrational and dangerous behavior. With this group of drugs, it is useful to record the number of prescription refills and the time interval between refills to see if the patient is increasing the dose or decreasing the dosage interval.

DISCUSSION AND IMPLICATIONS

Any psychotropic drug, whether prescribed or obtained in over-the-counter preparations, can result in inappropriate use by patients. This is of special concern with individuals with a prior history of drug abuse. The potential of the drugs listed in Table 1-3 to result in prescription drug abuse has been recognized by their inclusion under the Controlled Substances Act. These psychoactive drugs have been abused by health care providers, street drug abusers who come to physicians seeking a particular prescription, and patients who begin their use in the context of medical treatment. Each of these groups of psychoactive drug abusers needs attention if prescription drug abuse is to be eliminated.

Clinicians can make individuals in their care aware of the relationship between symptoms and their drug taking behavior focussing on both behavioral effects and physiological actions arising from numerous organ systems. It is useful to assess the nature of any health problems, in addition to the primary symptoms related to the addiction, that a client exhibits. These types of effects, as they ebb and flow with drug usage, may assist in patient recognition of the consequences of their drug taking and contribute to overcoming denial. Denial is often supported by the mythology that drug taking is not causing health problems yet, numerous symptoms may be exhibited or uncovered through careful history taking. Along with educating a patient on the numerous symptoms drugs may be causing, practitioners can use the disappearance of symptoms during drug abstinence, not only to reinforce the contention that drug taking was responsible for the health problems, but also to point out the healing process as it progresses. The general rule is that drug effects wear off and even long-time addiction to a drug should not be looked at as permanently damaging any organ systems. While the therapeutic process of dealing with the primary diagnosis of addiction may require prolonged treatment, many other drug-induced problems may disappear quite rapidly and the individual should be looked at as otherwise healthy not "damaged."

Physicians because of their role in prescription drug abuse need to understand the numerous issue involved in the addictions. As a consequence of drug abuse often being framed as a social problem rather than a medical problem, people, including physicians, develop opinions from information sources (media politicians, etc.) recognized to be unreliable for most medical problems. It will help to foster an appreciation that drug abuse is a large and continuously growing body of knowledge that can only be assimilated by some effort. It is important to recognize that while controversies exist, there is a great deal of consensus among prevention and treatment specialists that physicians can usefully convey to their patients.

Whenever a psychotropic drug is being prescribed there should be recognition and acknowledgement of that fact by the patient and prescriber. As a treatment plan is discussed prior to initiation of drug therapy, the subject of duration of psychoactive drug involvement should be included. Psychotropic drug indications are for medical conditions that are time-limited and amenable to nondrug interventions. Clearly, it is therapeutically beneficial to allow and encourage patients not to become dependent or abuse these psychoactive drugs. The ability to achieve this therapeutic goal is often compromised by a lack of knowledge particularly on the part of the patient.

There are numerous factors complicating elimination of prescription drug abuse. As mentioned, many specific drugs and drug categories are both therapeutic agents and street drugs. Furthermore, a great deal of information provided to the public has as its goal a decrease in psychoactive drug use rather than development of a chemically-literate population able to make rational health choices concerning all drugs. Aside from the wisdom of this approach to drug education, it results in a description of drug effects many of which are widely separated by dose and length of drug involvement. Little attention is paid to dose-response relationships (therapeutic dose to overdose) or duration of drug involvement (acute vs. chronic). All possible effects are often simply listed. This knowledge base is generally a poor starting point in allowing development of a treatment plan that the physician desires and the patient adheres to by choice. Finally, while there may be special ethical issues involved in the responsibility to insure that patients correctly use drugs that affect mind, attitudes, and thought, it will be difficult to achieve this with the current background of patient noncompliance across all categories of drugs.

REFERENCES

Akil, H. Watson, S.J. Young, E. Lewis, M.E. Khachaturian, H. and Walker, J.M. (1984). Endogenous opioids: Biology and function. *Annu. Rev. Neurosci., 7:*223–255.

Arnaud, M.S. (1987). *Prog. Drug Res., 31:*273–313.

Bloom, F.E. (1983). The endorphins: A growing family of pharmacologically pertinent peptides. *Annu. Rev. Pharmacol. Toxicol., 23:*151–170.

Brady, J.V. and Lukas, S.E. (Eds.) (1984). *Testing Drugs for Physical Dependence Potential and Abuse.* NIDA Research Monograph Series (No. 52). Rockville, MD: National Institute of Drug Abuse (U.S. Government Printing Office).

Congressional Record, *40:*102 (Part I), December 4, 1905 to January 12, 1906.

Cregler, L.L. (1989). Adverse health consequences of cocaine abuse. *J. Natl. Med. Assoc., 81:*27–38.

Cregler, L.L. and Mark, H. (1986). Medical complications of cocaine abuse. *New Engl. J. Med., 315:*1495–1499.

Duthie, D.J.R. and Nimmo, W.S. (1987). Adverse effects of opioids analgesic drugs. *Br. J. Anaesth., 59:*61–77.

Fischman, M.W. and Schuster, C.R. Cocaine self-administration in humans. (1982). *Fed. Proc., 41:* 241–246.

Gawin, F.H. and Ellinwood, E.H. (1988). Cocaine and other stimulants. Actions, abuse, and treatment. *N. Engl. J. Med., 318:*1173–1182.

Gengo, F.M. Huntoon, L. and McHugh, W.B. (1987). Lipid-soluble and water-soluble beta-blockers. Comparison of the central nervous system depressant effect. *Arch. Int. Med., 147:*43–59.

Gilman, A.G., Rall, T.W., Nies, A.S., and Taylor, P. (Eds.) (1990). *Goodman and Gilman's The Pharmacological Basis of Therapeutics (Eighth Edition).* New York: Pergamon Press.

Goldstein, A. (1984). Endorphins and Opioids. In Collier, H.O.J., Hughes, J., Rance, M.J., and Tyers, M.B. (Eds.), *Opioids: Past, Present and Future.* London. Tayler and Frances, Ltd. pp. 127–143.

Goudie, A.J. and Demellweek, C. (1986). Opioids and Behavioral Analysis. In Goldberg, S.R. and Stolerman, I.P. (Eds.) *Behavioral Analysis of Drug Dependence.* New York: Academic Press. pp. 225–285.

Griffiths, R.R., Bigelow, G. and Leibson, I. (1979). Human drug self-administration: Double-blind comparison of pentobarbital, diazepam, chlorpromazine and placebo. *J. Pharmacol. Exp. Therap., 210:*301–310.

Hughes, P.H., Brandenburg, N., Baldwin, D.C., Store, L., Williams, K.M., Anthony, J.C., and Sheenan, D.V. (1992). Prevalence of substance use among U.S. physicians. *J. Amer. Med. Assoc., 267:*2333–2339.

Isner, J.M., Estes, N.A.M., Thompson, P.D., Costanzo-Nordin, M.R., Subramanian,

R., Miller, G., Katsas, G., Sweeney, K. and Sturner, W.Q. (1986). Acute cardiac events temporally related to cocaine abuse. *New Engl. J. Med., 315:*1438–1443.

Kalant, H., and Kalant, O.J. (1971). *Addiction Research Foundation.* Toronto, Ontario, Canada.

Karch, S.B. and Billingham, M.E. (1988). The pathology and etiology of cocaine-induced heart disease. *Arch. Pathol. Lab. Med. 112:*225–230.

Katzung, B.C. (1992). *Basic and Clinical Pharmacology (Fifth Edition).* Norwalk, CT: Appleton and Lange.

Klein, D.F., Gittleman, R., Quitkin, F., and Rifkin, A. (1980). *Diagnosis and Drug Treatment of Psychiatric Disorders: Adults and Children (Second Edition).* Baltimore: The Williams and Wilkins Company. pp. 590–775.

Lawrence, C. (1988). *Congressional Quarterly,* pp. 3145–3151.

Martin, W.R. (1983). Pharmacology of opioids. *Pharmacol. Rev., 35:*283–323.

Matthys, H. Bleicher, B., and Bleicher, U. (1983). Dextromethorphan and codeine: Objective assessment of antitussive activity in patients with chronic cough. *J. Int. Med. Res., 11:*92–100.

McAuliffe, W.E., Rohman, M., Santangelo, S., Feldman, B., Magnuson, E., Sobol, A., and Weissman, J. (1986). Psychoactive-drug use among practicing physicians and medical students. *N. Engl. J. Med., 315:*805–810.

Multiple authors (1994). *Diagnostic and Statistical Manual of Mental Disorders, Fourth Edition.* Washington, D.C.: American Psychiatric Association.

Murray, R.M. (1978). The health of doctors: A review. *J.R. Coll. Physicians Lond., 12:*403–415.

NHSDA (1990). *National Institute on Drug Abuse. National Household Survey on Drug Abuse: Population Estimates.* Rockville, M.D.: U.S. Department of Health and Human Services (NIDA): U.S. Government Printing Office.

Ray, O. and Ksir, C. (1990). *Drugs, Society, and Human Behaviors.* St. Louis: Mosby. pp. 239–245.

Grabowski, J. (1984). *Cocaine: Pharmacology, Effects, and Treatment of Abuse* (NIDA Research Monograph Series No. 50). Washington, D.C.: National Institute of Drug Abuse (U.S. Government Printing Office).

Silverstone, T. (1986). Clinical use of appetite suppressants. *Drug and Alcohol Dependence, 17:*151–167.

Woods, J.H., Katz, J.L. and Winger, G. (1987). Abuse liability of benzodiazepines. *Pharmacol Rev., 39:*251–419.

Chapter 3

A TAXONOMY OF PRESCRIPTION DRUG ADDICTION

RAYMOND KRYCH, PHILIP H. WITT, AND ED FRANKLIN

INTRODUCTION

Although the occurrence of addiction to certain prescription medications has been recognized for quite some time, the actual incidence of this phenomenon remains unknown. Several recent studies have tried to examine this question and gather statistical data regarding the incidence of this problem in the general medical population, but hard data are limited (Busto, Sellers, Naranjo, Cappell, Sanchez-Craig, & Simpkins, 1986; Busto, Sellers, Naranjo, Cappell, Sanchez-Craig, & Sykora, 1986; Dupont, 1987, 1990; Griffiths & Roache, 1985; Griffiths & Sannerud, 1987; Owen & Tyrer, 1983; Senay, 1989; Tennant, 1987). In order to gain more information in this area, the present authors (Krych & Franklin, 1990) conducted a survey of 100 chemical dependence treatment centers in the state of Texas. All programs included in this survey provided chemical dependence treatment to adults age 18 and older. Fifty-one questionnaires were returned. Results of the survey revealed that between 5 and 10 percent of individuals seeking treatment at these facilities were addicted primarily to prescription medications.

More specifically, survey results indicated that prescription-addicted patients were primarily female (66.5% women; 33.5% men), while the general population of chemical dependence patients were primarily male (61.7% male; 38.3% female). Additionally, prescription-addicted patients generally were older adults (50 and older). The medications most commonly prescribed were benzodiazepines (50.3%), followed by narcotic analgesics (32.2%), then barbiturates (8.1%), stimulates (7.9%), and others (1.5%). Only two of the fifty-one treatment programs responding to this survey indicated they did not have any patients addicted to prescription medications in their patient population.

Clearly, there are large numbers of patients seeking treatment at

30

chemical dependence programs who are addicted to prescription medications.

While it may seem that these patients would best be served in treatment programs specializing in the treatment of addictions, in fact there is little available information regarding the nature of addiction to prescription medications, nor the best modalities of treatment for these patients.

Patients addicted to prescription medications differ from the more typical patients seeking chemical dependence treatment, and these differences must be considered when designing treatment strategies. For example, the substance abuse literature indicates that the majority of patients seeking treatment for alcoholism or drug dependence are males; however, the majority of patients in chemical dependence treatment who are addicted to prescription medications are females (Krych & Franklin, 1990). Furthermore, iatrogenically-addicted patients, as a group, are older than the general chemical dependence population. They tend to be older adults, primarily women, who began taking their medications (most commonly benzodiazepines or opiates) for relief of pain, anxiety, sleep problems, or depression.

TYPES OF PRESCRIPTION-ADDICTED PATIENT GROUPS

Based on a review of more than 200 patients in chemical dependence treatment who were addicted to prescription medications (of a total chemical dependence patient population of over 1600), there appear to be six distinct subgroups of these patients, each presenting a different clinical picture. Each of these groups presents special problems to be addressed in chemical dependency treatment. The groups are:

1. Pure Iatrogenic
2. Iatrogenic Pain Avoiders
3. Iatrogenically-Impaired Professionals
4. Iatrogenic Drug-Euphoria Motivated
5. Alcohol-Dependent Plus Prescription Medications
6. Street Drug Manipulators

Descriptions of each of these groups is given below.

1. PURE IATROGENIC

Core Characteristic: This group of patients consists of individuals who have

*used only the medications prescribed to them by their physician, and have
taken them exactly as prescribed.*

This group of patients consists of individuals who have used only the
medications prescribed to them by their physician, and have taken them
exactly as prescribed. However, after taking these medications for many
years (often 15 years or longer) these patients now find themselves being
instructed by their physician to "get off" these medications because they
have developed a physical addiction to them. Concerns of managing
possibly life-threatening withdrawal symptoms may prompt admission
to a hospital service, or, with increasing frequency in recent years, a
referral to a chemical dependence treatment program for medically-
managed detoxification and, occasionally, "treatment" and "rehabilitation."

Demographically, patients in this group are typically older (50 years
old and above) adults, and the majority are female. The most common
medications taken are benzodiazepines and opiates, often in combination
with various over-the-counter medications, some of which interact in
unanticipated fashion, producing a myriad of symptomatology. The
patient's concerns (or the patient's family's concerns) about these symptoms are frequently the very reason for the visit to the physician, and the
physician's subsequent decision to stop the medication usage. The prescribing physician becomes concerned about the extensive duration of
use of the medication by the patient. Another common scenario occurs
when a physician begins to treat a new patient and discovers the long-
term use of the psychoactive medications by the patient. In either case,
concern about complications of a possible withdrawal syndrome and/or
other harmful side effects of long-term use of the medication(s) (e.g.,
potential harmful interactions with other prescribed or over-the-counter
medications; concern about possible addiction) precipitates the physician's
decision to cease administration of the medication. Some physicians
conduct the detoxification themselves in a general medical hospital
setting. Others refer or admit patients to psychiatric facilities for the
detoxification, but increasingly physicians are referring their patients to
chemical dependence treatment centers to detoxification and rehabilitation.

Because this group of patients, primarily older women, have been
taking prescription medications as prescribed, typically from a family
physician they have known for many years, they are frequently shocked
to find themselves in a chemical dependence treatment center surrounded
by people with alcohol and/or drug problems. Often, they are confused
and even mortified.

A subgroup of the Pure Iatrogenic group consists of chronic pain patients. The effective management of the patient becomes more difficult if the underlying condition for which the patient was being prescribed the drug is a medical condition less amenable to psychological intervention. Chronic pain conditions are perhaps the most common examples (Portnow & Strassman, 1985), and accurately assessing the nature of an addiction problem in chronic pain patients is, quite often, extremely difficult. The most commonly found features in chronic pain patients addicted to prescription medications are as follows:

- simultaneous presence of both chronic physical pain and chronic psychological pain
- use of only prescribed medications, but often in amounts and frequencies greater than prescribed
- often, use of multiple prescription medications in conjunction with over-the-counter medications
- signs of physical dependence
- frequently, indicators of psychological dependence (drug-seeking behaviors, hidden use, preoccupation with taking medications, etc.)
- occasionally, these patients suffer from physical limitations and handicaps that complicate treatment
- occasionally, secondary gain is a prominent issue
- occasionally, alcohol use and/or abuse is a prominent issue, especially in males
- need for effective pain management, in many cases
- absence of Jellinek's signs of progression of addiction (Jellinek, 1960)

In some case, continued use of addictive medications is an appropriate treatment. The existence of an identified, destructive functional role of the medications in the patient's life is the primary indicator for determining whether or not the patient should remain on the medication. Tennant (1987), for example, has indicated that opioids are frequently necessary in treatment of chronic pain, and benzodiazepines in the treatment of chronic anxiety. If no effective means can be found to alleviate the pain, the patient is in a difficult position, forced to choose between a chemical addiction or unpleasant symptoms. In fact, some have coined the phrase "therapeutic addiction" (Tennant, 1987) to describe the situation when addiction to a prescription drug is the lesser of the evils. In any event, it is clear that some effective means for treating the patient's pain must be found in such cases.

2. IATROGENIC PAIN AVOIDERS

Core Characteristic: Individuals in this group have used only medications prescribed, but not as prescribed.

This is clearly the largest group of people addicted to prescription medications. Individuals in this group have used only medications prescribed, but not as prescribed. They typically have escalated their dosages beyond the dosages prescribed, and may have a number of prescriptions from numerous physicians (who usually are unaware of each other's prescriptions). However, they typically report that they primarily use medications to diminish or prevent perceived pain. It is important not to underestimate the strength of the patient's fear of perceived pain. The term "perceived pain" also includes unpleasant or uncomfortable psychological states, such as anxiety, frustration, depression, agitation, and anger, and so on, as well as actual physical discomfort. The anticipation of the return of perceived pain as the medications begin to wear off several hours after ingestion is often a fearful time for these patients, and triggers an almost panic-like reaction to take more medications before the pain/discomfort returns. Unfortunately, many of the prescription medications taken by these patients produce withdrawal symptoms that are very similar, if not identical, to the original disorders for which the medications were prescribed to treat (e.g., headaches, anxiety, insomnia). Pain Avoiders present special problems to treatment professionals. Unlike the Pure Iatrogenic patients, these Pain Avoiders, because they have a history of using more of their medications than were prescribed for them, have facilitated the development and ongoing progression of their addictions. Although they have abused their prescriptions, they nevertheless have great difficulty seeing themselves as "drug addicts" or "alcoholics," partially because they rarely if ever have used their medications to "get high." Furthermore, they often have developed an ingrained, long-standing life pattern of experiencing secondary gain due to being "sick and in need of medicine" (Walker, 1978), a phenomenon not found in most alcoholics/street drug addicts. Again, there are vast differences between this group of chemically-dependent persons and the "street addict," or as some have said, between the "medical addict" and the "criminal addict" (Walker, 1978). This difference in subculture and values must be taken into account in formulating treatment plans.

Issues regarding the format of chemical dependence treatment also present challenges when treating these patients. Most chemical dependence programs are oriented around Jellenik's "valley chart" (Jellinek, 1960) progression of the disease of alcoholism/drug dependence, and heavily involve the principles of AA and NA. In addition, group therapy is frequently the primary modality of psychotherapy in chemical dependence programs. Iatrogenic Pain Avoiders do not see themselves as experiencing the typical progression of alcoholism or drug dependence described in the "valley chart" model, and consequently often have great difficulty relating to other patients in treatment, and to AA and NA groups. In a sense, Iatrogenic Pain Avoiders have difficulty accepting the "enlightenment model" indigenous to these treatment approaches, in which the patient is seen as responsible for the escalation of the disorder but must surrender himself/herself to a "high power" for recovery to occur (see Brickman et al., 1982; Marlatt, 1988). More typically, these patients are compatible with a "compensatory model" in which they view themselves as not responsible for the elimination of their addiction (Brickman et al., 1982; Marlatt, 1988). Additionally, these patients, who are frequently older, often view chemical dependence (alcoholism and drug dependence) as a moral issue, and consequently as a perceived personal failing. Elderly persons, who constitute a significant percentage of this group, are very reluctant culturally to reveal personal information and/or perceived personal weakness in mixed-age group settings. Moreover, the use/abuse of prescription medications by elderly patients is not uncommonly an attempt to compensate for their own perceived age-related physical and psychological inadequacies and losses connected with the aging process. Revealing these ego dystonic inadequacies to other, younger alcoholics and drug addicts in group session is extremely threatening to these patients.

3. IATROGENICALLY-IMPAIRED PROFESSIONAL

Core Characteristic: This group is comprised of professionals in the health care field who have easy access to pharmaceutical medications and who begin to take these medications without true medical need.

Another group of individuals with addictions to prescription medications consists of professionals in the health care field who have easy access to pharmaceutical medications and who begin to take these medications without true medical need. In rare situations they may write prescriptions for themselves, but more commonly they simply use samples, or they steal medications from readily available supplies found in the medical setting in which they are employed. This group is primarily composed of physicians, nurses, pharmacists, dentists, students-in-training, and others who have relatively easy access to pharmaceutical drugs.

Some individuals in this group use pharmaceutical medications recreationally and develop an addiction to them, while others use the pharmaceutical drugs in a self-medication fashion (e.g., to relieve stress) and develop addiction. It is estimated, for example, that while the most common form of impairment in physicians is alcoholism (8% prevalence rate), nevertheless the second most common form of impairment for that group is drug dependence (McAuliffe et al., 1986; Nace, 1984).

For nurses, the rate of addiction to narcotics and other prescription medications equals that of physicians (Patrick, 1984). Pharmacists, dentists, and other professional groups are also acknowledging similar incidences of addiction to alcohol and psychoactive substances in their respective professions (Bissell & Haberman, 1984; Bissell, Haberman, & Williams, 1989; Brody, 1979). Bluestone (1986) presents a profile of the impaired nurse, indicating that they tend to:

- develop a dependence on chemicals as adults rather than as adolescents
- use chemicals initially for pain, fatigue or depression rather than to get high
- take drugs alone rather than with others
- obtain drugs through physicians, hospitals, and pharmacists rather than on the streets
- ignore or deny tension, depression, boredom, or unhappiness in themselves
- express guilt about their use of drugs
- hold demanding and responsible jobs
- be highly respected for excellent work that continues long after they begin to abuse drugs heavily.

4. IATROGENIC DRUG-EUPHORIA MOTIVATED

Core Characteristic: Members of this group gradually begin to use the prescribed drug not only to treat their medical disorder, but also to obtain an enjoyable intoxicated state.

Individuals in this group acquire their addictions initially through taking medication prescribed for them for relief from identified medical disorders. However, unlike the Pain Avoiders, members of this group gradually begin to use the prescribed drug not only to treat their medical disorder, but also to obtain an enjoyable intoxicated state. These patients rarely admit that they are using the drug for pleasurable effect — certainly not to their physicians or family members. Rather, they tend to exaggerate their physical symptoms in order to justify continued and sometimes escalating doses of their medications. Significantly, most of these patients do not use alcohol, even socially. This is the smallest of the groups, and it is primarily a pleasure-seeking group, with some elements of secondary pain, i.e., benefits of assuming the "sick" role, occasionally present.

Family issues are almost always critical with these patients. While these patients often present a "sick" role to their family members, effective treatment must help family members recognize that this is often a facade, a "pseudo-secondary gain." That is, the sick role is a means to an end for these patients, allowing them to hide their underlying desire to continue taking the medications in order to experience the intoxicating effect of the drugs. For most of these patients, the medical disorder for which the medication was originally prescribed had long since resolved.

5. *ALCOHOL DEPENDENT PLUS PRESCRIPTION MEDICATIONS*

Core Characteristic: These are patients who present at a chemical dependence program for treatment for their alcoholism, and in the course of treatment it comes to light that they are also abusing prescription medications.

Another group are those patients who present at a chemical dependence program for treatment for their alcoholism, and in the course of their treatment it becomes apparent they are also abusing prescription medications. These are not iatrogenically-addicted patients, but are supplementing their alcohol addiction with other psychoactive substances obtained through prescriptions from physicians.

These patients' motivation for taking the prescription medications may vary along the physical pain/psychological pain/pleasure seeking continuum. Some use the medications to potentiate the pleasurable effects of alcohol, while others may be using the medications to provide relief from physical or psychological pain or discomfort. A more thorough assessment of the functional role of the medications is necessary to provide effective treatment for these patients.

Patients in this group typically do not view their medications as addictive or problematic, and insist they have entered treatment to address only their alcohol use. Most individuals in this group who appear to be drug-euphoria motivated in their patterns of use typically deny this when initially confronted, but gradually acknowledge that this was the case.

6. *STREET DRUG MANIPULATORS*

Core Characteristic: Individuals in this group use prescription medications exclusively for the purpose of getting high on these substances.

Individuals in this group use prescription medications exclusively for the purpose of getting high on these substances. Unlike the iatrogenic drug-euphoria motivated group, however, individuals in this group did not acquire their addiction through treatment for a medical disorder, but rather included prescription medications in their repertoire of psycho-active substances.

This last group, therefore, is not truly an iatrogenically-addicted group, but consists mostly of alcohol and/or street drug addicts who manipulate physicians into prescribing medications to them. When in the physician's office, they will complain of blatantly fabricated symptoms specifically designed to obtain the desired prescription medications. It is said these patients know the effects (and side effects) of these medications better than their physicians. These patients also purchase prescription medications illicitly on the street and use them for their intoxicating effects.

Unlike the Iatrogenic Pain Avoiders and the Drug-Euphoria Group, individuals in this group of patients did not acquire their addictions as a result of treatment for a medical disorder, but rather they intentionally included prescription medications in their repertoire of psychoactive substance.

DISCUSSION

Individuals addicted to prescription medications constitute a significant percentage of patients seeking treatment at chemical dependence treatment centers. However, these individuals, while sharing some common characteristics, nevertheless can be differentiated into several subtypes, as described above. Some of these patients appear quite similar to traditional alcohol and/or drug abuse patients and would respond well to participation in most chemical dependence treatment programs (individuals in Groups 3 through 6). However, others, particularly individuals in the Pure Iatrogenic and in the Iatrogenic Pain Avoiders Groups, do not respond well to the treatment models widely prevalent today. The importance of matching these patients to the best course of treatment is predicated on the ability to differentiate between groups of patients.

An effective patient/treatment matching paradigm should lead to the development, implementation and evaluation of treatment strategies which address issues specific to patients in these identifiable subgroups. Optimal treatment for these patients requires therapeutic attention to both the initiating and maintaining functional components of the prescription medication usage.

REFERENCES

Bissell, L., & Haberman, P.W. (1984). *Alcoholism in the professions.* New York: Oxford University Press.

Bissell, L., Haberman, P.W., & Williams, R.L. (1989). Pharmacists recovering from alcohol and other drug addictions: An interview study. *American Pharmacy, 29,* 391–402.

Bluestone, B. (1986). *The impaired nurse.* Center City, MN: Hazeldon Foundation.

Brickman, P., Rabinowitz, V., Kazura, J., Coates, D., Cohn, E., & Kidder, L. (1982). Models of helping and coping. *American Psychologist, 37,* 368–384.

Brody, R. (1979). The story behind a pharmacist who got hooked on Rx drugs. *American Druggist, 179,* 32–36.

Busto, U., Sellers, E.M., Naranjo, C.A., Cappell, H., Sanchez-Craig, M., & Simpkins, J. (1986). Patterns of benzodiazepine abuse and dependence. *British Journal of Addiction, 81,* 87–94.

Busto, U., Sellers, E.M., Naranjo, C.A., Cappell, H., Sanchez-Craig, M., & Sykora, K. (1986). Withdrawal reaction after long-term therapeutic use of benzodiazepines. *The New England Journal of Medicine, 31*(14), 854–859.

DuPont, R.L. (Ed). (1987). Abuse of benzodiazepines: The problems and the solutions. *American Journal of Drug and Alcohol Abuse, 14* (Suppl. 1).

Dupont, R.L. (1990). Benzodiazepines and chemical dependence: Guidelines for clinicians. *Substance Abuse, 11* (4), 232–236.

Griffiths, R.R., & Roache, J.D. (1985). Abuse liability of benzodiazepines: A review of human studies evaluating subjective and/or reinforcing effects. In D. Lancaster (Ed.), *Abuse liability: Review of human studies* (pp. 209–225). Boston: MTP Press.

Griffiths, R.R., & Sannerud, C.A. (1987). Abuse of and dependence on benzodiazepines and other anxiolytic/sedative drugs. In H. Meltzer, B.S. Bunney, & J.T. Coyle (Eds.), *Psychopharmacology: The third generation of progress.* New York: Raven Press.

Jellinek, E.M. (1960). *The disease concept of alcoholism.* New Haven: Hillhouse Press.

Krych, R., & Franklin, E., Jr. (1990). *Incidence of iatrogenically addicted patients in chemical dependence treatment.* (unpublished presentation)

Marlatt, G.A. (1988). Matching clients to treatment: Treatment models and stages of change. In D.M. Donovan & G. A. Marlatt (Eds.), *Assessment of addictive behaviors* (pp. 474–483). New York: Guilford Press.

McAuliffe, W.E., Rohman, M., Santagelo, S., Feldman, B., Magnuson, E., Sobol, A., & Weissman, J. (1986). Psychoactive drug use among practicing physicians and medical students. *New England Journal of Medicine, 315*(13), 805–810.

Nace, E.P. (1984). Epidemiology of alcoholism and prospects for treatment. *Annual Review of Medicine, 35,* 293–309.

Owen, R. T., & Tyrer, P. (1983). Benzodiazepine dependence: A review of the evidence. *Drugs, 25,* 385–398.

Patrick, P. K. S. (1984). Self-preservation: Confronting the issue of nurse impairment. *Journal of Substance Abuse Treatment, 1,* 99–105.

Portnow, J. M., & Strassman, H.D. (1985). Medically induced drug addiction. *International Journal of the Addictions, 20*(40), 605–611.

Senay, E. C. (1989). Addictive behaviors and benzodiazepines: 1. Abuse liability and physical dependence. *Advances in Alcohol and Substance Abuse, 8*(1), 107–124.

Tennant, F. S., Jr. (1987). Clinical management of iatrogenic drug dependence. *Psychiatric Medicine, 3*(4), 337–347.

Walker, L. (1978). Iatrogenic addiction and its treatment. *International Journal of the Addictions, 13*(3), 461–473.

Chapter 4

CURRENT MEDICOLEGAL STATUS OF PRESCRIBING BENZODIAZEPINES: *A SPECIAL CASE*

Daniel P. Greenfield and Jeffrey A. Brown

> Most practitioners are aware of physicians in their commu-
> nity who will write prescriptions for benzodiazepines on request,
> even without examining patients (Applebaum, 1992).

We do not intend that the above statement from Applebaum set the tone for this chapter. We recognize that benzodiazepines (BDZ's) as a class of anxiolytic (antianxiety) psychoactive medication may have adverse effects (such as functional impairment, behavioral abnormalities, and physical and psychological dependence. Clinthorn, Cisin, Balter, *et al.*, 1986; Ray, Griffin, Donney, 1989). But perhaps more importantly, we also recognize and have concerns about the overshadowing in both the professional and public (lay) media of the therapeutic values of BDZ's by adverse publicity and out-of-context "horror stories." This has been the case recently for BDZ's (Greenfield, 1991) and other psychoactive medications (Greenfield and Brown, 1992), notwithstanding clinical and epidemiologic evidence that few patients prescribed BDZ's for legitimate indications become abusers of the drugs (Woods, Katz, Winger, 1988); that most BDZ users take these medications appropriately (Mellinger, Balter, Manheimer *et al.*, 1978); and that only a small proportion of individuals who use BDZ's—those with a predilection to abuse substances in general—appear susceptible to BDZ abuse (Ayd, 1990).

In keeping with the subject of this monograph, therefore, in this chapter, we will emphasize the clinical, medicolegal, and regulatory aspects of this widely-prescribed class of anxiolytic psychoactive medications as a current and often discussed "special case" of prescription drug abuse and dependence (PDAD). Specifically, we will review:

41

(1) Current clinical aspects of BDZ use and dependency;
(2) Legal and regulatory aspects of BDZ prescribing; and
(3) Practical guidelines for the safe and efficacious use of BDZ's

CLINICAL ASPECTS

In a previous publication, one of us wrote "... that physicians could be considered the gatekeepers to Paradise is unsettling ... " (Weiss and Greenfield, 1986) in terms of prescribing any psychotropic medications, and in terms of prescribing a particular subset of closely regulated psychotropic medications, namely "controlled dangerous substances" ("CDS," in legal terminology; see Chapter 1). Furthermore, in view of the increasingly negative publicity (Schneider and Perry, 1990; Greenfield, 1991) and the decline in use over about the past fifteen years (Alexander, 1988) of a major class of psychotropic medications, the benzodiazepines (BDZ's)—primarily agents for the treatment of anxiety disorders (Dilsaver, 1989; Cole, 1988), sleep disorders (Mendelson, 1987), and, more recently panic disorders (Upjohn, letter to physicians, 1990)—as a result of a variety of societal, medical, and related influences, the practicing physician is finding him/herself in an increasingly uncertain position with regard to prescribing these psychotropic medications. This situation is difficult when the physician is faced with clinical obstacles as well as with regulatory obstacles. An example of the former is the patient whose psychiatric symptomatology is a clear indication for treatment with psychotropics, but who is resistant to (and noncompliant with) this class of medications, or any other medications. An example of the latter is the regulatory issue over the past several years which places further restrictions and uncertainties (especially about potential disciplinary scrutiny) on the practicing physician's prescribing practices, namely that certain CDS medications with "abuse potential" be prescribed through multiple prescription documentation. While this requirement has existed for some time for psychotropic medications considered to have strong abuse potential (i.e., psychotropics "scheduled" as Schedule II under the Federal Controlled Substance Act (Comprehensive Drug Abuse Prevention and Control Act of 1970, 1970), it has been recently extended in one jurisdiction (as of this writing), New York State, to the benzodiazepines, which are themselves Schedule IV CDS drugs. The implication of this extension, therefore, is that the abuse potential of benzodiazepines is as great as that of Schedule II CDS agents (e.g., opiates), an implication that is at best questionable and at worst simply incorrect (Nagy, 1987).

In a thought-provoking paper, Taylor suggested that "there are two kinds of benzodiazepine dependence: a therapeutic and a morbid kind" (Taylor, 1989), thereby recognizing that dependence to benzodiazepines exists, but that not all such dependency is morbid, excessive, or "the opium of the masses" (Lader, 1978). The question of the extent to which benzodiazepines *are* abused by patients or prescribed to excess by physicians has been addressed extensively in the literature, with wide-ranging opinions expressed, from "too much," to "enough (Uhlenhuth, Demit, Balter, Johanson, and Mellinger, 1988), to "too little."

Realizing, however, that the psychiatric indications for which benzodiazepines are prescribed—anxiety, panic, and sleep disorders—are among the most prevalent conditions for which any psychopharmacotherapy can be useful, Uhlenhuth *et al.* (1988) make the following points:

"(1) The risk of dependence upon and addiction to benzodiazepines probably are remarkably low in relation to the massive exposure prevalent in our society. Certainly these risks appear to be lower than the current mythology holds and lower than the risks with other sedatives, such as barbiturates or alcohol.

(2) Systematic data confirms that benzodiazepine addiction can occur when doses even within the clinical range are taken regularly over a sufficient period of time, about 6 to 8 months. With fewer exceptions, however, even long-term users can discontinue benzodiazepines, if that is indicated.

(3) Some patients appear to derive continuing benefit from long-term treatment with benzodiazepines. Tolerance to the therapeutic effects commonly does not develop.

(4) Benzodiazepine over-use probably has been exaggerated. Indeed, the questions now seem to be rather whether attitudes strongly biased against the use of these drugs work to deprive the majority of severely anxious patients of appropriate treatment (Uhlenhuth, Demit, Balter, Johanson, and Mellinger, 1988)."

Taking into account, then, the *acceptability* of the notion that benzodiazepine abuse can and does exist, as does benzodiazepine dependence, practical clinical guidelines can be used to distinguish among these various types of benzodiazepine-taking behaviors. Table 4-1, for example, modified from Ayd, presents a useful series of comparisons between what Ayd terms "Benzodiazepine Medical Users and Nonmedical Users/ Abusers."

The distinctions made in this table underscore the common-sense clinical practices of prescribing *appropriate medications* (benzodiazepines) for *appropriate clinical conditions* (panic and anxiety disorders; sleep

**Table 4-1. Characteristics of Benzodiazapine Abusers and Users
(Modified from Ayd, 1987).**

	LEGITIMATE USERS	*ABUSERS*
I.	*Patient/Clinical Factors*	
	Generally established, known patients.	Often a new patient, unknown to the physician, from an unknown referral source.
	Generally accepts the physician's advice.	Often does not accept the physician's advice if it is not what s/he "wants to hear."
	Take only the benzodiazepine, generally as prescribed.	Usually abuse a number of drugs, more frequently than BDZ's, and often with BDZ's (especially sedating drugs)
	Present clear, or relatively clear, histories and complaints with indications (anxiety or sleep disorders) for BDZ's.	Present vague, nonspecific histories and complaints, with self-administration "to get high."
	More likely to be a woman, especially over age fifty.	More likely to be young, adult male, ages 20 to 35.
	Naive about BDZ's.	Knowledgeable about BDZ's; able to specify "the best medication for me."
	Generally keep scheduled appointments, follow instructions.	Often come as "walk-ins" or "emergencies" at the end or after office hours.
II.	*PHARMACOLOGIC FACTORS*	
	Usually take prescribed dose, or less.	Usually take excess dose.
	Generally do not develop a tolerance to BDZ	Often do develop tolerance, with progressive increases of dose to obtain the desired effect.
	Dislike sedative effects of benzodiazepines	Prefer and seek benzodiazepine effects.
	Rarely take more than 40 mg/day (or equivalent) of diazepam.	Often take more than 40 mg/day (or equivalent) of diazepam with progressive increasing doses (tolerance).
	Rarely at risk of severe withdrawal syndrome.	Often at high risk of severe withdrawal syndrome, including mixed (combined) sedative withdrawal syndrome from BDZ and concomitant other drugs.

Table 4-1. (Continued)

Generally keep scheduled appointment, follow	Often come as "walk-ins" or "emergencies" at the end or after office hours.

III. *CHEMICAL DEPENDENCY/DRUG ABUSE FACTORS*

Do not constitute a serious medical and/or social problem.	Often do constitute a serious medical and/or social problem.
Usually do not obtain BDZ's from "scrip docs."	Often obtain BDZ's and other prescription/CDS medications from "scrip docs," through diversion or theft from physicians, or through other illegal sources (Weiss and Greenfield, 1986).

disorders) at *appropriate dose levels* for *appropriate duration* for *appropriate patients* (i.e., nonabusers; Applebaum 1992). Extending this table as a prudent basis for the prescribing of benzodiazepines does provide a useful framework for judicious prescribing practices, both clinically and legally, for this useful class of psychotropic medications. This leads, logically, to the issue of the legal aspects of benzodiazepine prescribing.

LEGAL ASPECTS

On the level of personal health care (and prescribing practices), a good framework for the legal bases of prudent and judicious benzodiazepine prescribing is provided by Lesser in his paper entitled "Legal Issues and the benzodiazepines" (Lesser, 1989). In it the author deals with negligent aspects of tort law (i.e., professional liability, or malpractice), and lists the first seven of the eight areas of potential liability for physicians in prescribing benzodiazepines shown in Table 4-2.

These areas all apply to the legal theory of professional liability, or malpractice, which requires legal determination of a physician's *liability* with respect to prescribing, and also a legal determination of *damages* resulting from misprescribing (Crain, 1983).

Finally, with regard to the eighth point in the list, in view of increasing pressure and restrictions on physicians' prescribing of benzodiazepines, it behooves physicians to be aware of the latest medicolegal developments in that area. An unusual potential source of benzodiazepine litigation, for example, which has arisen in the United Kingdom recently

Table 4-2. Potential Areas of Professional Liability in Benzodiazepine Prescribing (After Lesser, 1989).

(1) History and examination (failure to perform these tasks adequately)
(2) Prescription of the wrong medication or the wrong dose
(3) Use for inappropriate duration
(4) Failure to monitor patient, to recognize, and to treat side effects
(5) Failure to anticipate drug-drug interactions
(6) Failure to consult with experts or to keep adequate records
(7) Withdrawal and discontinuation issues
(8) Lack of awareness of *unexpected,* not simply unusual, side effects

is that of alleged sexual impropriety of health care providers toward patients under the influence of benzodiazepines prescribed by physicians or other health-care providers, which influence further results in fantasies induced by the benzodiazepines. Brahams, writing in *The Lancet,* (Brahams, 1990) describes that situation as follows:

> Another unwarranted effect of benzodiazepines to surface recently is their potential to induce sexual fantasies in women... Prof. John Dundee... had details of 27 such allegations... When a follow-up of 2120 endoscopies and 900 dental operations done under local analgesia with diazepam or midazolam for sedation was published,... many more similar cases surfaced... and by December, 1989, another 15 cases had been brought... the total to 42... the fantasy-inducing qualities of benzodiazepines are only now being recognized, and in the past some doctors or dentists may have been wrongly convicted or disciplined for sexual offenses when the allegations stemmed from benzodiazepine-induced fantasies... (Brahams, 1990).

Regulatory Aspects: Multiple-Copy Prescription Programs (MCPP's)

On the level of public health care policy and regulation, we will next discuss a variant of CDS prescribing requirements unique to CDS, namely multiple-copy prescription programs, or MCPP's. Traditionally, such prescribing requirements applied only to drugs in Schedule II (see Chapter 1), the most carefully regulated and tightly monitored CDS schedule of drugs in common use by prescribers in the general health-care community. However, beginning on January 1, 1989, New York State law has extended triplicate (a variant of MCPP's) prescribing requirements to the benzodiazepines (still in CDS Schedule IV), and although to our knowledge, other states have not yet instituted similar MCPP's in their jurisdictions, there is great national interest in New York's BDZ prescribing "experiment," and other states may follow (Prescription Accountability Act of 1990, 1990).

In a "Report of the Board of Trustees" of the American Medical Association, Ring describes MCPP's as follows:

> In an effort to deal with prescription drug diversion, some states have adopted legislation that requires physicians to use special state-supplied two-or-three-part prescription blanks... for prescribing stipulated drugs (generally those in CDS Schedule II and certain analgesics in Schedule III). The blanks typically are preprinted with the prescriber's name, address, and DEA registration number, and are issued (generally for a fee) only to practitioners who are registered with the DEA and with the state, and who apply for the forms.

> When a prescription is issued on a multiple-copy form, the prescriber retains one copy (except in the case of duplicate-copy systems), and gives the remaining two copies to the patient. The patient surrenders both copies to the pharmacist, who retains one copy for file and sends the third copy to a designated state agency...

> Multiple-copy programs (also called "triplicate Prescription programs") currently are in place in seven states (California, Hawaii, Idaho, New York, Rhode Island, Texas), with legislation passed in two additional states (Michigan, Indiana) but the system is not yet operational (Ring, 1989).

According to DEA data, prescriptions for affected medications (mostly Schedule II) declined by 30 to 55 percent in the first two years of these programs (DEA, 1987). Regarding BDZ prescribing in New York State, prescriptions for BDZ's have declined by about 50 percent (Woods, 1990), raising the question of differentiating among prescription drug abuse, illicit drug abuse, and "legitimate" drug dependence (as described by Taylor).

To address this question, an American Medical Association (AMA) project (Ring, 1989) analyzed National Household Survey on Drug Abuse and Drug Abuse Warning Network data to investigate the following hypotheses:

(1) Diversion of prescription drugs for purposes of abuse is a significant contributor to this Nation's drug abuse problem and its attendant morbidity and mortality;

(2) Multiple-copy prescription programs are effective in reducing prescription drug abuse; and

(3) Multiple-copy prescription programs have *no negative effect* (emphasis added) on the availability of drugs for legitimate medical indications... (Ring, 1989).

The results of the AMA Report for that project supported the first hypothesis, but did not support the second and third hypotheses. The authors of that report concluded with the recommendation that the AMA Board of Trustees "oppose expansion of multiple-copy prescription programs to additional states or classes of drugs because of the documented ineffectiveness in reducing prescription drug abuse and their adverse effect on the availability of prescription medications for therapeutic use" (Ring, 1989).

More recent studies along these lines, but specific to the experience in New York State, have been done. These studies have examined how psychoactive medication prescribing patterns have been affected after one year of experience (January 1–December 31, 1989) by the triplicate prescribing requirement for BDZ's, based on data obtained through the National Prescription Audit (IMS America), New York State Medicaid, and Blue Cross/Blue Shield (Weintraub, Singh, Byrne, Maharej, Guttmacher, 1991). The studies investigated such questions as use of alternative psychoactive (anxiolytic, sedative, hypnotic, antidepressant, and other) medications as a substitute for less available (and less prescribed) BDZ's; changes in levels of BDZ prescribing and changes in expenditures for BDZ's and alternative medications.

With regard to the first two areas of investigation—the effects of the 1989 triplicate law on the prescribing of alternative medications—statistical results of the changes in frequency of BDZ's and alternative medications before and after the law are presented in Table 4-3. (These data are actually taken from the IMS National Prescription audit but are also representative of the Medicaid and Blue Shield/Blue Cross survey).

The dramatic decline in BDZ prescribing coupled with the equally dramatic increase in alternatives (not fully replacing the BDZ decline) led the authors of these studies to express concerns about the use of less safe and potentially more problematic alternative to BDZ's, such as barbiturates (Rall, 1990) and meprobamate (Roache and Griffiths, 1987): "The alternative sedative-hypnotic medications are less effective, more highly to be abused, and more dangerous in overdose than benzodiazepines," (Weintraub *et al*, 1991). The authors also expressed concern about undertreatment of clinically significant anxiety, panic disorders, or insomnic: " . . . an unknown part of the decrease in prescribing may have been achieved at the expense of legitimate use." (Weintraub *et al*, 1991). From the financial perspective, although the authors of these studies acknowledge that there has been a decline in BDZ prescribing as a result

Table 4-3. Representative Changes in BDZ and Alternative Medications
after the 1989 N.Y.S. Triplicate Prescribing Law
(IMS National Prescription Audit Data (after Weintraub et al., 1991).

Drug	% Change Nationally (1988–1989)	% Change in N.Y.S. (1988–1989)
Benzodiazepines	−9%	−51%
Alternatives		
*Meprobamate	−9%	+125%
*Methylprylon	−15%	+84%
*Ethylchlorvinyl	18%	+29%
*Butabarbital	−15%	+31%
*Hydroxyzine	−1.1%	+15%
*Chloral Hydrate	−0.4%	+136%
*Buspirone	−	126% (Medicaid data)

of the new law, "there has been no overall change in expenditures for psychotherapeutic agents . . . ," (Weintraub *et al*, 1991) and that because of the complexity of evaluating the risk-benefit ratio attendant to clinical situations resulting from the N.Y.S. triplicate BDZ prescribing law, ". . . how much money is really being saved (or wasted) by the health care system as a whole . . . " (Weintraub *et al*, 1991) is difficult to assess.

SUMMARY AND CONCLUSIONS

The widespread use of benzodiazepines has been a source of concern and debate, due in large part to the traditional association of "mood-altering" or sedating drugs with problems of abuse and dependence. Such problems have indeed been reported with the benzodiazepines, and the view has emerged that abuse and dependence might account for a substantial proportion of benzodiazepine use. On the other hand, many investigators have found that most use of benzodiazepines is appropriate to the prevalence of the medical and psychiatric conditions for which they are deemed effective. Physicians prescribing these drugs are faced with the need to weigh the potential risk to their patients against the drugs' demonstrated benefit in the treatment of anxiety and insomnia (Woods, Katz, and Winger, 1988).

Woods, Katz, and Winger (1988) have provided the above statement in their State of the Art Review article; this statement both characterizes and summarizes the points and controversies raised in this chapter. In terms of concrete and practical aspects of benzodiazepine prescribing, the following several points from this chapter can be made by way of summary:

(1) Benzodiazepines have an important place in the pharmacotherapeutic treatment of anxiety, insomnia, and panic disorders (mainly), and of psychological responses to medical conditions and other disorders (secondarily). With prolonged benzodiazepine prescribing, however, some proportion of patients can be expected to become dependent on these medications, with "Non-medical Users/Abusers" (and those with a history of such abuse) (Ayd, 1987) showing a greater frequency of dependence than "Medical Users" (Ayd, 1987).

(2) The principles of prudent and judicious prescribing of benzodiazepine's are essentially the same as those of prescribing of any other class of medications. However, the psychoactive nature of benzodiazepines makes it essential that the prescriber be aware of possible side effects (including unusual ones such as the induction of sexual fantasies by benzodiazepines; Brahams, 1990), in order to treat appropriately and avoid, if possible, even the remotest likelihood of inappropriate or negligent prescribing.

(3) Multiple-copy prescription programs are problematic: Generally, the physician has to prescribe within the MCPP guidelines, where they apply (i.e., whether for Schedule II for all states with MCPP's, and for benzodiazepines [Schedule IV CDS drugs] in New York State), recognizing that " ... The aim of societal controls is not only to restrict the availability of those substances for abuse, but to do so without restricting their appropriate medical use" (Woods, 1990). This goal is at best problematic in the ways in which these MCCP programs attempt to meet them, and has been the source of a good deal of controversy and debate over the years (Farnsworth, 1991).

Finally, although we agree that "Clinicians must be mindful of the risk of dependence when prescribing benzodiazepines and in light of the ethical dictum to do no harm, must avoid practices that increase that risk" (Noyes, Garvey, Cook and Perry, 1988), we are also mindful that the disorders of anxiety, sleep, and panic all have high prevalence in the general population (DuPont, 1986). The benzodiazepines have a definite place in psychopharmacologic aspects of the treatment of these disorders and can be safely, efficaciously, and judiciously prescribed, keeping in mind the clinical and legal principles described in this chapter. The final point of which we are also mindful is that public health policy, such as that of prescription drug diversion, abuse, and dependence—which MCPP's are supposed to address—should not deprive the public of useful medications and that such policy should "protect rather than jeopardize the public health" (Woods, 1990).

Endnotes

(1) Although beyond the scope of this chapter, for a concise overview of classes, indications, side effects, dose ranges and other such clinical prescribing aspects of the benzodiazepines, see Hindmarch *et al.* (1990).

(2) For a more detailed discussion of the legal principles underlying professional liability ("malpractice"), especially the "four D's" of (1) *Duty* to treat; (2) *Dereliction* in that *Duty*, resulting in; (3) *Damage* to the patient, which is the; (4) *Direct*, or *"proximate"* cause of that Damage, See Crain (1983).

REFERENCES

Alexander, P. (1988). The clinical and scientific rationale for tapering benzodiazepines. Kalamazoo, Michigan: The Upjohn Company.

Applebaum, P. (1992). "Controlled Prescription of Benzodiazepines," *Hospital and Community Psychiatry, 43:* 12–13.

Ayd, F. (1990). "Benzodiazepines: medical users vs. nonmedical users/abusers. *International Drug Therapy Newsletter, 25:* 8.

Brahams, D. (1990). Benzodiazepines and sexual fantasies. *The Lancet,* 335: 157.

Clinthorne, J., Cisin, I., Balter, M. *et al.,* (1986) Changes in popular attitudes and beliefs about tranquilizers. *Archives of General Psychiatry, 43:* 527–532.

Comprehensive Drug Abuse Prevention and Control Act of 1970, 21 *U.S.C.* 812 (b) 2 (c).

Cole, J. (1988). The drug treatment of anxiety and depression, *Medical Clinics of North America, 72:* 815–830.

Crain, P. (1983). Civil Law. In Talbott, J.A. and Kaplan, S.R. (Eds.), *Psychiatric Administration,* NY: Grune & Stratton.

DEA, Multiple Copy Prescription Program Resource Guide (July, 1987), Washington, D.C.: U.S. Drug Enforcement Administration.

Dilsaver, S. (1989). Generalized anxiety disorder. *American Family Physician: 39,* 137–144.

Farnsworth, P. (1991). Personal Communication, May 20, 1991.

Greenfield, D. (1991). "What about Halcion?," *New Jersey Medicine, 88:* 889–890.

Greenfield, D., & Brown, J. (1992). "What about Prozac?" *New Jersey Medicine, 89:* 445–446.

Hindmarch, I., Beaumont, G., Brandon, S., Leonard, B., *Benzodiazepines: Current Concepts, Biological, Clinical, and Social Perspectives* (1990), N.Y.: John Wiley and Sons.

Lader, M. (1978). Benzodiazepines: the opium of the masses. *Neuroscience, 3:* 159–165.

Lesser, I. (1990). Legal issues and the benzodiazepines. *American Journal of Forensic Psychiatry, 10* (4): 5–13.

Mellinger, G., Balter, M., Manheimer, D., *et al.,* (1978). "Psychic distress, life crisis, and use of psychotherapeutic medications: National household survey data. *Archives of General Psychiatry, 35:* 1045–1052.

Mendelson, W. (1987). Pharmacotherapy of insomnia. *Psychiatric Clinics of North America, 10:* 555–563.

Nagy, A. (1987). Long-term treatment with benzodiazepines: Theoretical, ideological, and practical aspects. *Acta Psychiatrica Scandinavica, 76 (suppl. 335):* 47–55.

Noyes, R., Garvey, M.J., Cook, B.J. and Perry, P.J. (1988). Benzodiazepine withdrawal: A review of the evidence. *Journal of Clinical Psychiatry, 49:* 382–389.

Prescription Accountability Act of 1990, HR 5530, 101st Congress, Second Session, 1990.

Rall, T. (1990). Hypnotics and Sedatives: Ethanol (pages 345–382), in Gilman, G., Rall, T., Nies, A., Taylor, P. (Eds.), *Goodman and Gilman's The Pharmacologic Basis of Therapeutics, Eighth Edition.* N.Y.: Pergamon Press.

Ray, W., Griffin, M., Downey, T. (1989). Benzodiazepines of long and short elimination half-life and the risk of hip fracture. *Journal of the American Medical Association, 262:* 3303–3307.

Rifkin, A., Doddi, S., Karajgi, S., Hasan, N., and Alvarez, L. (1989). Benzodiazepine use and abuse by patients at outpatient clinics, *American Journal of Psychiatry, 146:* 1331–1332.

Ring, J. (Ed.) (1989). Report of the board of trustees: curtailing prescription drug abuse while preserving therapeutic use—recommendations for drug control policy. *Journal of the American Medical Association, 262:* 1–12.

Roache, J. and Griffiths, R. (1987). "Lorazepam and meprobamate dose effects in human behavioral effect and abuse liability, *Journal of Pharmacology and Experimental Therapeutics, 243:* 978–988.

Schneider, P. and Perry, P. (1990). Triazolam—an abused drug by the Lay Press? *DICP, The Annals of Pharmacotherapy, 24,* 389–392.

Taylor, F.K. (1989). The damnation of benzodiazepines. *British Journal of Psychiatry, 154:* 697–704.

Uhlenhuth, E., Demit, H., Balter, M., Johanson, C. and Mellinger, G. (1988). Risks and benefits of long-term benzodiazepine use. *Journal of Clinical Psychopharmacotherapy, 8:* 161–167.

Upjohn Company, letter in November 1990 (to all physicians, announcing F.D.A. approval of alprazolam (Xanax) for pharmacologic treatment of panic disorders).

Weintraub, M., Singh, S., Byrne, L., Maharej, K. and Guttmacher, L. (1991). Consequences of the 1989 New York State triplicate prescription regulations, *Journal of the American Medical Association, 266:* 2392–2397.

Weiss, K. and Greenfield, D. (1986). Prescription drug abuse. *Psychiatric Clinics of North America, 9* 475–490.

Woods, J., Katz, J. and Winger, G. (1988). Use and abuse of benzodiazepines. Issues relevant to prescribing. *Journal of the American Medical Association, 260:* 3476–3480.

Woods, J.H. (1990). Abuse liability and the regulatory control of therapeutic drugs: untested assumptions. *Drug and Alcohol Dependence, 25,* 229–233.

Chapter 5

INTERVIEWING THE DIFFICULT PATIENT

DANIEL P. GREENFIELD AND JEFFREY A. BROWN

> In the medical interview, typically, one person is suffering
> and desires relief; the other is expected to provide this relief.
> The hope of obtaining help to alleviate his suffering moti-
> vates the patient to expose himself and 'tell all.' This process
> is facilitated by the confidentiality of the doctor-patient
> relationship. (MacKinnon and Michaels, 1971).

Ordinarily, the paradigm of the clinical interview, as described above,
forms the basis of the therapeutic "contract" between clinician
(therapist, counselor, physician, psychologist, etc.) and patient (client,
consultee, etc.). It also describes the basis of the ongoing therapeutic
relationship of those two individuals: One individual perceives that
he/she needs therapeutic help, and seeks that help through another
individual who is perceived as having the expertise to provide that help
(Lazare, 1982). Even allowing for some degree of distortion in the initial
reporting of problems and noncompliance in therapy (Podell, 1975), this
basic model of the clinician-patient is the core of that relationship. A
basic assumption in that model is of *honesty,* on the part of both clinician
and patient, toward each other in that relationship.

In the case of difficult (Lipsitt, 1970), disturbed (Kahana and Bibring,
1965), "hateful" (Grove, 1978) or manipulative patients, however, this
model is changed—even "perverted," according to some (McGough,
1985). In these situations, a patient's ulterior motives toward a health-
care professional, whether they are for secondary gain (Engel, 1962),
conscious malingering (Cavenar and Brodie, 1983), or other reasons,
present a muddied picture to the health-care provider in terms of what
"relief" (MacKinnon and Michaels, 1971) the identified patient seeks.
The range of these possible reasons is enormous, and a discussion of that
range is beyond the scope of this chapter.

However, *one* reason from this range of possibilities for a patient's duplicitous presentation to a health-care professional of a suffering and desires for relief may be drug-seeking, specifically *prescription* drug-seeking (see Chapter 3 for a discussion of taxonomy of prescription drug seekers). In this chapter, we will use that reason, described in a case example, as a basis for a discussion of the initial encounter of the health-care professional with such a drug-seeker — "interviewing the difficult patient."

CASE: A DRUG-SEEKING PATIENT

Dr. K., a 32-year-old married family physician and amateur basketball player, had been in his suburban practice for four years; he was closing his office at about 3:00 P.M. on a Saturday, already annoyed that he was two hours late for a family basketball outing over the coming holiday weekend. When he was just about to leave, a young man (late twenties) dressed in a suit and tie who identified himself as "Tom . . . Tom Collins" appeared at Dr. K's office as a walk-in patient. "Tom" stated that he was a salesman by profession, recently hired as a local American representative for a company based in England, who lived in a distant (out-of-state) city. He had been referred to Dr. K. by his own physician (in that distant out-of-state city). Dr. K. did not know "Tom's" doctor, and did not later find him listed in the current *Directory of Medical Specialists,* even though "Tom" described him as "a very good, qualified, board-certified cardiologist," whose first name, address, and telephone number "Tom" had forgotten. "Tom" said that his physician referred him to Dr. K. because of Dr. K.'s presumed reputation as " . . . a good guy . . . a good doctor . . . he really cares about his patients" (presumably, "Tom's" physician's statements). "Tom" wanted to see Dr. K. because he had "lost the other doctor's prescription," and he was re-experiencing complaints of "migraine headaches . . . they're on my left side, and I get nauseous with them, and see lights on the left . . . ;" complaints of " . . . pain and cramps in my stomach and bloody diarrhea- . . . from my colitis . . . that's in my family, too . . . ;" and complaints of "knife-like excruciating back pain . . . from my car accident three years ago . . . they were going to do a laminectomy for a herniated disc, but they decided not to, so I've been living with the pain ever since . . . " Before Dr. K. finished taking the history, Tom grabbed his head, wincing and bending forward in pain, describing that he was having a migraine attack, and asking for "a shot of one hundred milligrams of Demerol . . . that's the only thing that works when I get these attacks . . . and if you won't give me that, give me six two-milligram Dilaudid . . . they'll probably work, too. Nothing else works — Talwin, Darvon, Fiorinal, Naprosyn. I've tried them all and they just don't work. (While Dr. K. was away from his interview room, he glimpsed at Tom, and noticed that he was calmer and did not appear to have a headache).

After completing the history, which Tom resisted giving and which resulted in the above information, Dr. K. told Tom that he wanted to do a physical examination. Tom refused initially, saying "Doc, I know what's wrong with me and what I need. They say you're a good doctor—you care. Why don't you just give me what I need? I know it'll work. If you don't give it to me, I'll have to get it somehow...maybe even on the street. You'll be forcing me to do that. Or maybe I can get some DL's [Dilaudid] from another doctor...I've done that before...and I've gone into hospitals sometimes, too. Doc, let me pay you for this visit with cash (showing a thick roll of twenty-dollar bills)—how much is it? Just name your price. Maybe that will make it easier for you to give me what I need..."

Dr. K. refused to prescribe anything unless Tom allowed the rest of the interview, the physical examination, and a witnessed random urine drug screen (U.D.S.) to take place. Tom refused all of these therapeutic interventions, and stormed out of Dr. K.'s office angrily, muttering under his breath, "I just don't need him...I'll get fixed...I'll get the stuff somewhere...he can go to..."

As we described at the beginning of this chapter, prescription drug abuse (and dependence), or PDAD, is a particularly egregious example of the misapplication of the clinician-patient relationship and its basic tool, the clinical interview. Such tasks of the interviewer as information gathering, establishing of rapport, enhancing patients' self-esteem, facilitating a productive discussion, developing a therapeutic contract, and other related tasks do not occur, because the purposes of the interview have been usurped by the only goal of the PDAD "patient"—to obtain drugs. Although national surveys suggest that PDAD is declining (DAWN, 1988–1991), other data indicate that about 3 percent of all prescribed psychoactive drugs are diverted, one way or another, from the presenting health-care provider (Wilford, 1990). Therefore, it behooves health-care practitioners—especially those who can prescribe psychoactive medications and scheduled medications ("Controlled Dangerous Substances," or "C.D.S." (Weiss and Greenfield, 1986) themselves—to be aware of and skillful in interviewing and evaluating the PDAD "patient," as well as other difficult patients. These areas will be discussed below.

Assessing the Context

In the case described above, a number of the hallmarks of the PDAD patient's presentation is seen. Table 5-1 (adapted from Powell, 1989) lists some of these features.

The case presented above includes a number of examples of points raised in the guidelines in Table 5-1. Other features in the case which

Table 5-1. Guidelines For Detecting The Drug Seeker
(after Powell, 1989)

---

(1). Early warning signs
  - Patient/client from a distance away
  - Multi-organ system and multi-site pain
  - Vague personal history and identification
  - Comes to the office off-hours
  - Requests specific medications during first visit
  - Claims of lost or stolen prescription

(2). Later signs
  - "Conning," manipulative, or overly abusive behavior
  - Offers to pay for services in cash
  - Resists physical examination and urine drug screen (U.D.S.)
  - Resists efforts to contact previous prescriber

---

also should have raised Dr. K's suspicions that this patient may have been seeking drugs included his lack of involuntary autonomic features associated with pain; the observation that the patient appeared agitated when seen (the "pain show," Vilensky, 1983), but quiet when not seen; and the fact that the patient was unable to remember specifics about his own physician (in the distant city). In evaluating (and treating) patients in this situation, or in any situation in which the questions may arise of a patient's, possible ulterior motives, several principles of interviewing should be understood.

First, the interviewer should have a high *index of suspicion* that the patient may have ulterior motives in seeking help from the interviewer. The PDAD patient is a particularly noteworthy example of this possibility. Clues about this type of patient's motives can be seen in Table 5-1, and in Tom's case. Other attitudes or behaviors for non-PDAD patients or clients, in extreme form, are exemplified in Groves' taxonomy of four stereotyped types of "hateful" patients, namely "dependent clingers," "entitled demanders," "manipulative help-rejecters," and "self-destructive deniers" (Groves, 1978). In less flagrant situations, the interviewer's index of suspicion about a client/patient's ulterior motives may be raised by his/her complaining about previous therapists; by his/her presenting vague (and untreatable) complaints and symptoms; by his/her unwillingness to discuss sensitive topics at appropriate times (". . . that's too personal . . ."); by his/her presenting issues of possible secondary gain (MacKinnon and Yudofsky, 1988), as a justification for seeking treatment

("... my wife said that if I got into counselling she'd leave me alone ... ");
and others—the list could be endless!

Second, the interviewer should be aware of his/her own developing
and evolving general emotional responses as well as *countertransference*
("... responding to aspects of the patient as if [she/he] were an important person from the [interviewer's] past...." (MacKinnon and Yudofsky,
1988) responses to the patient/client. This can be an important piece of
data to the interviewer, especially in situations in which a countertransference response is negative, and similar to a response to a "difficult"
person in the interviewer's own experience.

Third, in a similar vein, the interviewer should be aware of the
client/patient's developing and evolving general emotional responses as
well as his/her *transference* ("... the patient unconsciously and inappropriately displaces on to persons in his current life those patterns of
behavior and emotional reactions that originated with significant figures
from [his/her past] ..." (MacKinnon and Yudofsky, 1988) responses to
the interviewer. Analogous to the countertransference situation, important data can be obtained through understanding the transference, especially in situations in which the interviewer ostensibly "brings out"
difficult characteristics in the client/patient "... just the way my father
used to do ... "

Fourth, and last for present purposes, the circumstances, or context, of
the interview should be understood. Is the client/patient being interviewed
voluntarily (e.g., self-referred, referred by another health-care provider,
referred by a friend or colleague because of an honest need for evaluation and/or treatment, etc); involuntarily (e.g., court-ordered, involuntary hospitalization/civil commitment, etc.); or "quasi-voluntary" (e.g.,
required for discharge planning from an involuntary hospitalization,
required as part of a child custody dispute, etc.)? All of these circumstances may have important implications regarding the client/patient's
motivation for the interview and for subsequent treatment. Again, the
PDAD patient is an extreme example of an unusual circumstance for an
interview: In that circumstance, the interview is "quasi-voluntary," and
may even be "forced" by the patient's need to obtain psychoactive substances to avoid withdrawal and to support his/her drug habit.

BEGINNING THE INTERVIEW

Implicit in the description of Dr. K's behavior in his interview with "Tom Collins" is the notion of *control* during the interview. No clinician would want to regard a client/patient encounter *a priori* as adversarial in nature, with effective communication blocked because of "ground rules" inherent in such encounters (Quill, 1989). However, in situations in which the clinician's "index of suspicion" indicates that the patient may have ulterior motives—as Dr. K. suspected early on in his interview with "Tom"—it is essential for the clinician to control the interview situation. In doing so, the clinician must make it clear to the patient that the clinician will not go beyond the limits of the clinical context, and will only treat the patient according to his/her usual and customary professional practices. (In Dr. K's and "Tom's" case, this meant, among other things, Dr. K's refusal even to consider prescribing for "Tom" unless he agreed to have a physical examination and urine drug screening [UDS]. As a result, Tom realized that he would not be able to manipulate or "con" Dr. K. into prescribing for him, so he left). In this vein, Goldman points out that although it may seem difficult to "just say no" to patient, *not* to do so is a disservice to clinician and patient alike (Goldman, 1987).

A pleasant, neutral, and firm approach to a clinical interview, in our experience, is a useful and productive one, and is also one which is best suited for clients who may have "ulterior motives" when they are being interviewed.

Once clarification of the roles of the interviewer and the patient has been established, and through that clarification, control by the interviewer also established, the tasks of the rest of the interview can be addressed. Briefly, those tasks include establishing rapport, facilitating a productive discussion, enhancing patient/client's self-esteem, gathering information (obtaining a history), developing a therapeutic contract, providing information and instructions, and giving feedback and answering patient's/client questions (Froelich and Bishop, 1977). Useful techniques at this early phase of the interview with difficult patients— including PDAD patient/clients—are limit-setting, maintaining a technically neutral posture and demeanor, and—again—maintaining control, among others. These tasks and techniques can be difficult to accomplish with difficult and resistant patients, as was the case with Dr. K. and "Tom." In that case, Dr. K.'s main task was to identify "Tom's" true motivation for being interviewed (to obtain drugs), and to act appropriately (by not prescribing for him), which he did.

CONTINUING THE INTERVIEW

At this point during the interviewing, a distinction between *diagnostic* and *therapeutic* interviewing ought to be made. In the former case, potentially antagonistic feelings between the interviewer and the patient may develop, as the patient/client may sense that she/he is " . . . a specimen of pathology being examined" (MacKinnon and Yudofsky, 1988), particularly with the expectation that a longer term (than one or two interview sessions) will not develop. The challenge in this situation of developing rapport with patients especially difficult and resistant ones, is great. Even in the case of difficult patients, if the patient's motivation is not *honest* — as was the case with "Tom" — rapport and a therapeutic environment will be extremely difficult to achieve.

Assuming that even a difficult, or resistant patient, has some degree of motivation for treatment, the interview will continue, at this early point, into the information-gathering (obtaining a history) phase. At this phase, however, and throughout the interview, the interviewer of the difficult patient must remain aware of the patient's resistance and lack of cooperation — for whatever reason or reasons; must make allowances for his/her own reactions (emotions and countertransference) to these problems; and must maintain a neutral therapeutic environment to the extent possible. Dr. K's frustration and anger at the time he was refusing to prescribe anything for "Tom" are examples of these points.

At the information-gathering phase, the interview can be broadly divided into two parts, i.e., the history and the mental status examination.

A sample "medical model" format of a history, adapted from MacKinnon and Yudofsky (1988, page 37), is presented in Table 5-2.

Although a detailed review of these and other related topics is beyond the scope of this chapter, we emphasize two points in the context of the difficult client/patient: (1) The systematic review and business-like questioning of client/patients — even resistant ones — in obtaining a history with a format such as that presented in Table 5-2 can be extremely useful in "defusing" potentially volatile interview situations and in maintaining neutrality; and (2) on the other hand, even attempting in such a professional and business-like manner to obtain a history can be an aggravating

**Table 5-2. The Psychiatric History
(after MacKinnon and Yudofsky, 1988)**

1. Preliminary identification
    (a) Reasons for referral
    (b) Chief complaint
    (c) Identifying information
2. History of present illness
    (a) Onset; precipitating factors
    (b) Secondary gaine
3. Psychiatric and medical history and review of systems
4. Personal history
    (a) Prenatal history; pregnancy factors
    (b) Early Childhood (early; middle; later)
    (c) Psychosocial history
    (d) Religious, cultural, and moral background
    (e) Adulthood (occupational; military; academic; social; sexual; and so forth)
5. Family history

and trying experience for the interviewer. Again, the interviewer must be aware of his/her emotional and countertransference responses to this difficult situation, and adapt accordingly.

Similar to obtaining a history, the mental status examination part of the interview should be undertaken in a neutral, professional, and straightforward way; a sample format, also adapted from MacKinnon and Yudofsky (1988), is presented in Table 5-3.

A detailed review of this format is also beyond the scope of this chapter, but we note again that the two points made above in connection with obtaining a history (above) also apply in connection with performing a mental status examination. (For a discussion of psychological testing and related procedures with PDAD and other difficult patients, see Chapter 6: "Clinical Interviewing and Psychological Assessment of the Prescription Drug Abuser).

CONCLUDING THE INTERVIEW

At this point, assuming that the "difficult patient" has not left the interview, has agreed to further interviews and in some instances to testing procedures, understands the nature and purpose of this interview, and has agreed to such requirements as permitting the collateral inter-

**Table 5-3. The Mental Status Examination
(after MacKinnon and Yudofsky, 1988)**

A. Appearance, attitude, and behavior
  1. General description (clothing; hygiene; etc.)
  2. Behavior; psychomotor activity
  3. Attitude toward examiner and interview/examination
  4. Speech (structure and content)
B. Thought process and content
  1. Production and continuity of thought
  2. Content of thought and perception
    (a) Preoccupations and obsessions ("neurotic-level")
    (b) Delusions; illusions; referentiality; and other perceptual distortions
    (c) Depersonalization and dissociative phenomena
  3. Abstract and concrete thinking
  4. Concentration; memory; orientation cognition;
     attention; and other cognitive functions
C. Affect, mood; and emotional regulation
  1. Subjective evaluation (mood)
  2. The interviewer's observations (affect)
D. Higher Cognitive functions
  1. Information and intelligence
  2. Judgement
  3. Insight

viewing of family members and friends, the interviewer should now conclude the interview, always maintaining control (particularly important with difficult and resistant patients).

Here, the tasks of the interview in providing feedback and answering questions are important, and in our experience can provide useful closure to the interview itself. Specifically, after the "diagnostic" (history and mental status examination) parts of the interview are complete and a discussion of goals of the evaluation or the treatment plan (if applicable) are nearly complete, the interviewer can end the discussion of goals, and s/he can then discuss practical aspects of the interview (such as scheduling a follow-up appointment, discussing additional referrals or consultations or tests, and so forth). At that point, it should be clear to both the interviewer and the patient if a rapport has been achieved and if a therapeutic relationship begun, and if future sessions will occur. If the relationship is to continue, then the interviewer should leave a brief but reasonable period of time for questions from the patient and for feedback from the patient. In the latter context, we have found the following question of patients a particularly useful "invitation" for feedback: "Is there anything else about you which I should know at this point?" If the relationship is *not* to continue, the interviewer should discuss future treatment plans or options with the patient, such as referral to other health-care providers or facilities, the adverse consequences of *no* treatment or intervention, and the continuing availability (if true) of the interviewer "in case you (patient) change your mind." If the relationship is not to continue and the client/patient leaves precipitously (as "Tom" did), in our opinion, the interviewer should still make efforts to provide information about referral and treatment to the departing patient. Since chemical dependency (including PDAD) is so often characterized by exacerbations and remissions, relapses and recovery, and "slips" and sobriety, the "way back" to recovery should always be pointed out to the client/patient. Put in another way, " . . . some positive statement concerning the doctor's belief that the patient will recover is part of the therapy" (MacKinnon and Yudofsky, 1988) and—in our judgment—part of the interview process, even with "difficult patients."

SUMMARY AND CONCLUSIONS

Prescription drug abuse and dependence (PDAD) patients can be very difficult to interview and—when applicable—to treat. In this chapter, we have provided an overview of interviewing difficult client/patients, from the perspective of the interviewer (the clinician) and the interviewee (the patient). In keeping with the theme of this monograph, we have used the PDAD patient as the paradigm of the "difficult" patient, and have particularly focused on signs, symptoms, "clues," and other features of the PDAD patient to assist the clinician/interviewer to identify such individuals. We have emphasized, however, that the PDAD patient is only one relatively small example in the universe of "difficult" patients—an admittedly extreme example. We have also provided practical formats and pointers for interviewing other difficult patients, as well as ways to understand—to some extent—and work with such patients in an interview situation.

As we stated at the beginning of this chapter, the clinical interview is the cornerstone for evaluation and treatment of patients. Ordinarily, *honesty* is the basis of the understanding or therapeutic contract between clinician/interviewer and patient. Many patients can be "difficult" for a variety of reasons: fear, anger, underlying personality, and so forth, and the PDAD patient can be the most difficult of all because of the *dishonest* reasons for his/her seeking professional attention. However, those patients can be identified and treated under some circumstances, using the principles and pointers described in this chapter. We recommend that the interested clinician attempt to work with such patients, since even though they can be difficult and frustrating for the clinician, they are chemically dependent individuals desirous of help to some extent. In addition, as this monograph has emphasized in a number of contexts, the only real difference between PDAD individuals and other chemically dependent individuals is the way in which the former obtain their drugs of abuse.

REFERENCES

Cavenar, J. and H. Brodie (Eds., 1983). *Signs and Symptoms in Psychiatry.* Philadelphia: J.B. Lippincott.

Drug Abuse Warning Network (1988–1991) (Statistical Series, Series 1, Numbers 8, 9, 10, 11), Washington, D.C.: U.S.D.H.H.S. (National Institute on Drug Abuse).

Engle, G., (1962). *Psychological Development in Health and Disease.* Philadelphia: W.B. Saunders, pp. 225–227.

Froelich, R. and F. Bishop. *Clinical Interviewing Skills (Third Edition).* St. Louis: C.V. Mosby.

Goldman, B. (1987). Confronting the prescription drug addict: Doctors must learn to say no. *Canadian Medical Association Journal, 138:* 871–878.

Groves, J. (1978). Taking care of the hateful patient. *New England Journal of Medicine, 298:* 883–887.

Kahana, R. and Bibring, G. (1965). Personality Types in Medical Management (pages 108–123), in Zinberg, N. (Ed.), *Psychiatry and Medical Practice in a General Hospital.* N.Y.: International Universities Press.

Lazare, A. (Ed.) (1982). *Outpatient Psychiatry Diagnosis and Treatment* (1982). Baltimore: Williams & Wilkins.

Lipsitt, D. (1970). Medical and psychological characteristics of "crocks." *Internal Journal of Psychiatry in Medicine., 1:* 15–25.

MacKinnon, R. and Michels, R. *The Psychiatric Interview in Clinical Practice* (1971), N.Y.: W.B. Saunders, p. 5.

MacKinnon, R. and Yudofsky, S. (1988). *The Psychiatric Evaluation in Clinical Practice,* Philadelphia: J.B. Lippincott, pp. 17–18, 12–13.

McGough, W., Personal Communication, November 14, 1985.

Podell, R. (1975). *Physicians Guide to Compliance in Hypertension,* Rahway, N.J.: Merck.

Powell, K. (1989). The drug seeker: Where do Health Professionals Stand?" *Current Therapeutics, 30:* 67–68, 73–75.

Quill, T. (1989). Recognizing and adjusting to barriers in doctor-patient communi-
    cations. *Annals of Internal Medicine, 111:* 51–57.
Vilensky, W., Personal Communication, April 5, 1983.
Weiss, K. and Greenfield, D. (1980). Prescription Drug Abuse, *Psychiatric Clinics of
    North America, 9:* 475–489.
Wilford, B. (1990). Prescription Drug Abuse. *Western Journal of Medicine, 152:* 609–612.

Chapter 6

CLINICAL INTERVIEWING AND PSYCHOLOGICAL ASSESSMENT OF THE PRESCRIPTION DRUG ABUSER

PAMELA E. HALL

INTRODUCTION

The psychological assessment of the prescription drug abuser is an area of clinical focus which demands far more attention than the limited amount of information available to date. There still exists no preferred specific protocol for the assessment of such patients. This is also true for the assessment of alcoholics and other chemically-addicted individuals.

The diagnosis of substance abuse is one often made by patients themselves and/or family members in many instances. These are the individuals ravaged by the pain and heartache that is the disease of chemical dependency. It is not unusual to hear a patient or family member saying "he/she has a drug or drinking problem . . . " It is because the diagnosis of substance abuse can often be made in this manner, without psychological assessment, that many clinicians and patients alike may wonder what assistance such formal assessment can offer.

The psychological assessment of the chemically-dependent patient or prescription drug abuser can help to formulate the focal point of treatment planning for the addictive patient. The following chapter is designed to shed new light on the concept of psychological assessment for the prescription drug abuser and chemically-addicted adult. These suggestions are based upon several years of clinical experience in the field of substance abuse and supervisory work with talented, motivated, and often recovering Certified Alcohol Counselors and staff.

GENERAL CONCEPTS ABOUT
PSYCHOLOGICAL ASSESSMENT

Psychological assessment usually involves a two-tier process. The initial phase is that of the clinical interview. It is preferable that this preceed any formal testing efforts in order to establish rapport and provide a framework by which the patient can describe their past substance abuse history to the best of their ability. The second phase of assessment usually involves some sort of formalized testing.

Psychologists are trained in a variety of testing instruments which may offer additional insight into a patient's level of functioning. These tests include instruments that measure intellectual functioning, gross and fine motor coordination, and elements of organic impairment and/or subtle signs of brain damage, both related or unrelated to the chemical addiction. Additional tests, referred to as projective testing, assess personality style, identify defense mechanisms typically employed by the patient, and highlight psychodynamic and emotional issues that may have a strong impact on the patient's level of self-esteem or general motivation toward recovery.

It is preferable for every patient to receive a full battery of psychological tests; however, due to time management and financial constraints, this is not always possible. It is recommended that each patient be given a minimum of an extensive clinical interview and a general assessment device (such as the MMPI) to screen for dual diagnosis issues early on in the treatment process. Testing efforts should begin once the patient has been fully detoxed and is committed to a full program of treatment for chemical dependency.

It is essential that patients receive full and proper feedback about the results of their psychological testing. It is poor clinical practice to conduct testing and not give such feedback. Patients are often left feeling exposed after a testing experience. This unearths some basic anxieties about their mental health, etc. even for the healthiest of patients. The testing process also generates much curiosity about one's personal general mental health which should be addressed and discussed with the patient directly. It is an opportunity to build upon the natural curiosity of the patient and is a time in treatment when they will be the most reflective and open to feedback. If the chance for communicating about test results passes, the individual often becomes more closed than before because they have co-operated and opened themselves up without any personal gain.

The feedback of test results should be provided by the same professional who administers the testing procedures when at all possible. This is critical when a full battery has been administered involving tests which require training in interpretation. There are some test profiles which can be scored electronically and an interpretive report can be obtained. It is essential to realize that computer-generated reports are not for patient consumption. It is advisable that a professional trained in testing procedures still be the one to provide the feedback from the report. The language utilized by such services is unfamiliar to most patients and only serves to be either useless or upsetting if patients review the reports without professional psychological guidance to ensure proper interpretation of the findings.

THE CLINICAL INTERVIEW

There is much useful information to be gleaned from the clinical interview because patients are far more able to provide a picture of their substance abuse than any formal assessment tool yet devised. This fact remains despite their denial, minimization, and ... yes ... even when presenting a falsehood. The clinician well-trained in clinical interview skills, who also possesses a working knowledge of substance abuse, will be able to discern some of the fact from fiction; however, the most important factor is the patient's realization of his or her own efforts at mispresentation. This realization challenges the addict, who is fully aware of his or her efforts to conceal the truth, and remains a very powerful clinical intervention.

It is imperative to note that the clinical interview should serve a dual purpose. The obvious purpose is to obtain factual information that will assist the clinician to make a diagnosis of chemical addiction as well as identify ongoing areas of emotional need. The second purpose of the interview, however, is the most important but perhaps the least obvious. This interview is an opportunity for the patient to begin to study and question his/her own behavior in depth, often for the very first time. When a clinician hears his/her patient say something akin to "I never realized this, but now that I'm hearing myself talk ... ," this is the most reliable indicator that treatment has indeed begun! It is quite possible for patients to undergo a full rehabilitation program, even several programs, and still not be able to internalize the responsibility and develop the insight necessary for long-term successful recovery.

Sparking the patient to think about his/her own issues in addiction is the beginning of effective treatment. When the psychologist or clinician can foster a sense of self-examination and personal responsibility in the patient through the clinical interview, treatment is enhanced and the therapeutic messages given by other counselors in the treatment effort are reinforced. This is in keeping with the goal of multidisciplinary treatment for addiction which is often the treatment of choice for patients with addiction issues.

Guidelines for Conducting the Clinical Interview

(1) **Approach:** The material to be obtained from clinical interview should be gathered in as little an invasive process as is possible. This serves to minimize denial and other defense mechanisms common in addiction. It is recommended that the interviewer begin by asking some general questions about the patient's everyday life and present circumstances. Essential details of the patient's social and familial interactions are usually easily accessed. It is critical to determine how the patients have been obtaining their supply of chemicals/prescriptions and what techniques they have used in the past. This is not only helpful to the clinician, but the patients are immediately directed to focus upon, and recognize, their own patterns of use and the manipulation they employ to obtain their drug of choice.

(2) **Analyzing patterns:** The addiction cycle sets in motion a complex set of circumstances which must become known to the therapist. Many a patient has relapsed, not due to lack of knowledge about recovery, but due to extenuating factors in the patient's life unknown to the therapist at the time of the treatment effort. One of the clearest examples of this phenomenon is the all-too-often minimal attention given to family history. For example, if a woman is a victim of sexual abuse by a family member who is still in close contact with her (as is often the case), relapse to addiction will most likely occur despite the best of therapeutic interventions. Until the issues of establishing safety and autonomy for the patient are addressed, chemical addiction will usually persist without relief.

Recently, there has been a tremendous awareness of the patterns of codependency and ACOA (Adult Child of Alcoholic) issues which exist in family members and in addicts alike. A detailed discussion of these issues is beyond the scope of this writing, however, the clinical interviewer should be aware that this consciousness has added a valuable new dimension to addiction treatment because both the therapist and patient can finally begin to isolate and reconstruct new patterns of behavior for the addict "where they live" which is in their family setting. It is expecting a lot of patients to maintain an undaunted level of commitment to sobriety and recovery while being bombarded by powerful cues of unchanging family "values" and "messages." These well-defined roles potentially pull the addicted person back into the synergic whirl of family dynamics and results ultimately in relapse.

Hospitalized patients are temporarily shielded from such entropic forces, nevertheless, it is most beneficial when these patterns can be discovered in the clinical interview. They are to be identified, carefully assessed and then communicated to the patient, if they are to ever gain mastery over such dynamics for long-term recovery. A common example of such powerful family synergy is the recovering patient who excelled throughout rehabilitation and then returns home only to become suicidal and actively using substances within a few short weeks or even days,

(3) **Directives for treatment:** The clinical interview can serve to spot such difficulties early in treatment rather than waiting for such material to emerge in the context of group therapy or risk that such issues may not be uncovered at all in the treatment effort. The benefit of early detection is that strategies for change and coping can be designed and even employed by the patient while they are in an inpatient or intensive outpatient program. Successful interventions can be reinforced, while corresponding reactions of guilt and fear can be ameliorated.

Family sessions can then be better targeted to specific issues of benefit to the patient rather than focused solely on general family bonding, confrontation, etc. The clinical interview can be most beneficial also in pinpointing the essentials of individual therapy contact while the patient is in treatment. Special concerns to be addressed at the time of termination can also be identified from the moment of initial contact. This approach will ensure a comfortable transition for the patient to autonomous living again. Frequently, the necessary "social services" aspects of a patient's life are left unresolved or pending further arrangement upon discharge from inpatient or intensive outpatient care. Immediate assessment of discharge/termination issues should be part of the initial clinical assessment. Not only does this give staff more time to coordinate and arrange services, but patient's resistance or fears to follow their discharge plans can be addressed as part of the ongoing therapy effort.

(4) **Addressing social/emotional needs:** This arena is usually handled in treatment by suggesting that patients reconstruct a new set of peers and friends which share the same recovery background and experiences. While this is a valid and necessary adjustment, patients will often struggle greatly with this expectation. They are being required to sometimes sever relationships that they perceive mean a great deal to them. It is best if the areas of risky social relationships be discovered during the clinical interview process. In this way, the interviewer can assist the patient and other counselors to begin the process of selecting appropriate friendships early on in the phase of treatment and recovery. Unresolved high-risk relationships are a major component in relapse and a threat to successful treatment. In some cases, there are high-risk individuals, such as family members, who cannot be totally cut off from contact with the addicted person. In these instances, it is paramount for therapy to address coping strategies for dealing with this reality as soon as possible during the course of therapy.

The chemically-addicted patient and/or prescription drug abuser may deny any difficulties in the area of social functioning. They are often misleading, appearing far more relaxed in social contexts than they are in actuality. The clinical interview can be used to assess to what extent the individual is suffering from social anxiety or possibly an undiagnosed social phobia for which they have been using drugs/alcohol as a compensatory device.

(5) **Vocational needs:** Many individuals have developed the need for prescription drugs/alcohol to assist them in functioning on their job. The most familiar example of this is the truck driver who begins to pop pills to stay alert on the road or the entertainer who employs a combination of medications to go to sleep and wake up at odd hours of the day and night.

The clinical interview must determine such practices for two reasons. First, prescription addicts will often believe that such methods are acceptable as long as an important purpose is involved, like working. This must be confronted at the outset of treatment. Second, it may be necessary to assist the patient to decide whether or not to return to his or her vocation at all. In some cases, it will be possible for them to face the job without the need for drugs in the future, for others they may need to retool for new work because they must admit they cannot return to the same work environment without relapse.

Patients with other forms of chemical addiction will be pressured with the cultural aspects of the job and coworkers. Common examples are laborers who celebrate a hard days work with some beers or the business man or woman who is confronted with the traditional "business luncheon." This event, which usually entails taking clients for drinks, is difficult and sometimes impossible to avoid in certain lines of work. Special survival/coping strategies must be formulated with the patient as soon as possible, particularly in outpatient treatment. Dialogue about alternatives to present employment must also be addressed as a viable option.

In situations where retooling is necessary, there are state and local social services which can be of valuable assistance. State sponsored vocational rehabilitation services can offer vocational assessment and individual counseling. In some states they may also provide for private psychotherapy relevant to vocational issues such as low self-esteem, sobriety management, assisting in deciding a new direction for work, etc. They also may assist to place individuals in certain jobs. This may be particularly useful for dually-diagnosed clients who may be unable to compete in the open job market. In addition, some of the jobs available through the state tend to be less high pressured, although they also pay accordingly.

(6) **Aspects of spirituality:** The clinical interview should address aspects of the patient's spiritual background and upbringing as well as his/her present-day position on the matter. It is quite often that these two perspectives differ greatly from one another.

Many individuals identify with a specific religious affiliation; however, life events or personal decisions have often alienated them from their childhood faith practices. Since this is a common occurrence, most adults do not recognize alienation from spirituality as a problem related to their addiction. It is essential to explore the history of spirituality with ALL patients, even those without any spiritual orientation, in order to determine possible areas of strength or untapped spiritual resources that might assist in the recovery process.

A typical example of being alienated from one's spirituality of the past might be a young woman who had been a devout Catholic as a child but became pregnant in young adulthood and obtained a subsequent abortion. As a result, she alienated herself from the church, stopped attending services, and spent much time walking around with a feeling of low self-worth as a "sinner" and estranged believer. Another example might be a middle-aged businessman who was raised by his parents close to the Jewish faith, but since their death and a series of disillusionments in his own life, has ceased any religious practices and struggles with fear of his own death and the existential pain of middle age. A final scenario might be an individual who has had no religious upbringing and chooses not to follow any such philosophy. They can feel distaste for the spiritual lingo of the anonymous recovery process encouraged by many treatment programs.

All of these individuals need a clinician willing to discuss their spiritual orientation. The clinician must be accepting of ALL spiritual processes and religions, and not be threatened by discussing such matters. This will best be accomplished if the clinician realizes that their job is NOT to provide any spiritual advice or direction, but rather to assist patients in exploring their own existential issues and discover how to reengage the beliefs and practices that have given them comfort or respite in the past. Exploration of religious guilt and encouragement to seek resolution of such issues is an essential part of any complete therapy process.

In consideration of the individual who chooses to include no religious perspective, they must be assisted to obtain other avenues of relief from guilt, resentment and existential issues via a method they either develop individually or with therapeutic assistance. The task of the clinician conducting an initial interview is to highlight these issues for the client by questioning in this area; a full resolution of such problems is not possible or even expected in this phase of contact. There are many patients who fail in recovery because they are repelled by the "religious" aspects they perceive in Alcoholics Anonymous. As a result, they are also unfortunately deprived of the important socialization, peer support, and alcohol/drug free events offered by the program at no cost. If such realities are not discovered with the patient in the initial interview, there will be no opportunity to address the patient's distaste during treatment.

It should also be noted that for believers and nonbelievers alike, a patient's annoyance about the spirituality aspects of self-help recovery can become another convenient excuse why he or she cannot engage fully in recovery process. As a therapist, one cannot shy away from exploring EVERY aspect of human life including subjects such as sex, spousal abuse, child abuse, AIDS, fears, fantasies, and religion/spirituality as well.

(7) **Aspects of personal or societal risk:** It is essential to assess the potential suicidality and homicidality of every patient in addiction.

Specifically, prescription drug abusers may be self-medicating undiagnosed major depression or manic depressive tendencies. Once the addiction aspect of their presenting problem is addressed, they will be confronted with the biochemical realities of their depression diagnosis. In such a situation, along with successful abstinence may come increased psychiatric risk for possible suicide. Attention should be devoted in the initial interview to such feelings of depression and a clear determination of suicidal risk must be specified in an effort to alert other primary staff of the need for ongoing monitoring of suicidal ideation when appropriate. In order for suicidality and depression to be properly assessed, it is essential for the clinician to have well developed knowledge-base about psychiatric illness.

Homicidal ideation, while admittedly less common, is still a critical issue to explore in the initial interview. Clinicians will often refrain from such questions in an effort not to alienate the patient. They may feel foolish asking a prominent businessman or a professional woman about such thoughts and often struggle with an acceptable way to even word such an inquiry. The issues of homicidal ideation is an essential part of the traditional mental status exam and with good reason. As mental health providers, an accurate assessment of a patient's mental health includes his/her attitudes about relationships to other people, both in his/her family and society at large. There is a certain inherent obligation for us to examine such possible risks of homicide and it is not valid to certify a certain level of mental status without properly investigating same.

In addition to the duty of examining such tendencies for the benefit of the patient and the safety of society, such questioning, if done properly, can be very useful clinically, even when the patient is not homicidal in the least. The clinician can begin to explore such thoughts by first asking about how the patient handles aspects of frustration in his/her life. This will lead directly into a discussion of difficult life events. Anger is an essential issue to address in recovery and will naturally flow from a discussion of how to handle frustration. At this point the clinician should ascertain the patient's level of frustration tolerance. In cases where it appears that the individual has a solid grasp on anger issues, it is still appropriate to question whether or not they have ever felt angry enough to actually want or plan to hurt another person, then requesting them to explain how they handled those impulses. This should clarify the extent of their ability to mediate such impulses.

When it is determined that a patient exhibits low frustration tolerance and/or poor judgment in situations of anger, further exploration is indicated. The interviewer should continue to engage the patient in discussing how they rectify such events in their life. If the solution is apparently maladaptive, that is via physical violence or rage, the clinician can serve as the first reality check for the patient and should express concern that this is not an acceptable method to resolve conflict. It is only through such lines of questioning that issues of abuse can ever be uncovered and interventions can be offered.

In instances when a patient does exhibit homicidal ideation, whether it be due to psychosis or irrational angry tendencies, it is crucial to determine if there is any specific person on whom they focus their anger and blame. Appropriate steps to warn such identified parties must take place immediately, as well as efforts to arrange for hospitalization of the patient for more intensive psychiatric evaluation and treatment. It is now becoming common knowledge that a large portion of violent crimes and homicides include alcohol and drug addiction as a primary causal factor. The prescription drug addict is less likely to manifest homicidal ideation, however, spousal abuse and/or child abuse may very likely be part of their addictive behavioral repertoire.

(8) **Overall mental status:** The clinician should next be able to offer an overall impression about the mental status of the individual and a sense of their ability to engage in the treatment process waiting at the next juncture. The patient's level of motivation and his/her capability for insight should be specified. The general psychological health of the person versus the issue of a dually-diagnosed patient should be distinguished in the first assessment session. Since dually-diagnosed patients have a corresponding mental disorder, the clinical evaluation phase must serve as a screening mechanism to flag such clients for ancillary or separate services tailored to meet their specific needs.

(9) **Treatment recommendations:** The initial assessment phase is the critical point of intervention which will decide what services a patient will receive often throughout the rest of the treatment effort. The reason for conducting such a comprehensive evaluation is in order to be able to determine accurately all the treatment issues to be addressed. In essence, the clinician is designing a template for the treatment effort to follow, whether that be individual therapy or a multidisciplinary treatment team. In today's cost-conscious managed care scene, the effective and decisive evaluation of substance abuse patients is only becoming more

imperative. An extra effort applied at the outset of treatment will bear out many advantages for both patient and therapist long-term. There are numerous approaches and factors in the treatment of substance abuse which will be addressed in another chapter. It is the initial evaluation which will hopefully dictate a clear method of how to proceed with each new patient.

Treatment recommendations are essential, but it is also helpful if the clinician can address a wide range of patient needs. Psychological assessment and other means of formalized testing can often assist in this process. In many cases, formal test results can help the clinician understand some profound motives for the substance abuse or shed light on possible reasons for chronic relapse, etc. Some uses of assessment tools will also be discussed in this monograph.

(10) **Medication needs:** The clinician conducting the initial assessment phase may often be a psychologist or other mental health professional that does not prescribe medication. Despite this fact, the clinician should address the issue of medication needs via a recommendation for full psychiatric evaluation when appropriate. This is yet another screening function of the initial interview process which, if done properly, can eliminate the treatment failures of the past when such dual-diagnosed patients were not properly identified.

It is important for the clinician to have a positive attitude about both the recovery and psychiatric cultures. If the clinician doing the initial evaluation imposes his or her personal treatment biases upon the assessment, the patient will be the likely victim. While the recovery culture is often "anti-meds," it is still valid that certain patients do require, and cannot recover, without the assist of psychiatric intervention. Likewise, talk therapy may be a potent tool in the recovery process, but it too, is not the only resource to be offered or required. The assessment should be able to specify and identify these differences at the outset of treatment.

ASSESSMENT TOOLS

There are some assessment tools employed in the field of substance abuse which are specific to the realm of addiction. Other instruments are "generic" types of psychological tests in that they are employed to assess all types of patients in the general psychiatric population and even utilized in the general population as well. The following discussion will sketch an outline of various types of tests with specific mention of particularly useful or popular devices. It should be noted that self-report instruments and various assessment scales often do not require any specialized training for interpretation. Tests of a psychological nature, however, do dictate that the interpreter be professionally trained in order to properly interpret the results of the test and be able to glean accurate conclusions from the data.

SUBSTANCE–ABUSE ASSESSMENT TOOLS

(1) The CAGE questionnaire (Ewing, 1984; Mayfield, McLeod & Hall, 1974) is a direct and helpful way in which to focus on four primary factors in the assessment of alcoholism. These same questions can be most useful with regard to the prescription drug abuser. Not only will this focus assist the clinician to make a determination of addiction, but the mere exploration will induce the patient to begin to question his or her drug usage.

The acronym, "C–A–G–E" represents the following items:

C—cut down: This questions whether or not the patient has ever been directed to cut down on their use for alcohol (or in this case, prescription drugs previously prescribed).

A—annoyed: This explores the patient's level of anger or annoyance when someone comments on their substance use.

G—Guilt: This focus addresses any sense of personal guilt felt by the patient for events that occurred while drinking, or in the case of the prescription drug abuser, for the extensive lying or manipulation they may have orchestrated to obtain their drug of choice.

E—Eye-opener: This addresses the need for alcohol, (or drugs) in the a.m. This can be expanded to include the craving for the drug at any time of day or night.

(2) The MAST (Michigan Alcohol Screening Test, Selzer, 1971) and DAST (Drug Abuse Screening Test; Chappel, J., presented at lecture to the National Judicial College on Alcohol and Drugs: "Handling User Abuse Cases," Princeton, July 7, 1986).

These are two of several checklists available to assist in the diagnosis of chemical dependency. The advantages of such tools are that they are self-administered and take relatively little time to complete. There is no specific training required for interpretation. The questions described particular behaviors which patients are challenged to admit. The very description of familiar behaviors begins to set in motion the confrontation aspect of the treatment process for the patient as they recognize their own behaviors in the questions.

These are drawbacks to the use of such instruments. A major consideration is that it is easy for patients to misrepresent the severity of their problem through fake responses which do not report their actual behavior (Hester & Miller, pg. 23). Despite this fact, the very direct questioning nature of these instruments is confrontive and, therefore, of clinical value in the diagnostic process.

(3) MODCRIT: This is modified version of the CRIT (Criteria) for the diagnosis of alcoholism which was published by the National Council on Alcoholism in 1972. The MODCRIT shaves the original 85 question instrument down to 36 signs of addiction administered in 30–40 minutes. Some of the questions can be used as a template for the prescription drug abuser, but the reliability and validity must not be assumed when questions are altered for such purposes.

(4) The Mac Andrew Scale: This is most commonly recognized as a subscale of the MMPI (Minnesota Multiphasic Personality Inventory), however, the MAC can be administered independently. Developed by MacAndrew, the scale claims to identify a pattern of responses similar to patients with present or even future alcoholic tendencies. These same tendencies are found in the drug abuser as well.

(5) The MMPI, used in its entirety, does require specific training to properly interpret all the scores, but is a most useful tool in the initial phase of addiction treatment for several reasons. The test is entirely self-administered; yet, with the inclusion of the Mac Andrew scale the questions about addictive tendencies are better concealed than in most other self-report questionnaires. In addition, the MMPI offers an interpretive profile generated by computer which can provide the basic analysis of personality style and addiction potential for use by any clinician in the treatment program. The MMPI results will render a solid sense of the patient's personality style and offer some insights into possible areas of treatment impasse or resistance. The pattern of responses will clue the clinician into the possibility of a dually-diagnosed

individual if certain scores are notably elevated. This test addresses the mental status of the patient in both an overall and specific manner. It is a most useful tool for the beginning phases of treatment. The nature of the questions usually sparks some curiosity in the patient to receive feedback "about their personality." This opens the door for further exploration, discussion and confrontation about the issue of addictive tendencies. It gives patients concrete feedback about their personality style while giving clinicians some quantifiable numerical scores to consider.

PSYCHOLOGICAL ASSESSMENT TOOLS

Psychological tests can be extremely helpful in understanding aspects of a patient in addiction. Although they require a trained psychologist to administer and interpret the results, the data obtained lends itself to a more thorough assessment of the patient and will ensure an accurate treatment plan as a result.

A psychological screening battery may include some of the following tests:

Intellectual Evaluation

The most widely used tool for assessment of intelligence is the WAIS–R (Wechsler Adult Intelligence Scale-Revised). This is a comprehensive test with sound reliability and validity ratings. The WAIS–R yields an IQ or Intelligence Quotient which has become known world-wide. The WAIS–R has also been found to assist in determination of the extent of Korsakoff's syndrome and other organic factors of addiction (Anastasi, p. 467–471).

While patients' level of intellect should always be considered, intelligence testing can also be helpful in identifying possible areas of learning disability and/or organic factors that may have occurred as a result of long-term addiction. It provides a breakdown of a patient's areas of strengths and weaknesses. This is extremely useful in treatment planning because areas of untapped strengths, as well as cognitive limitations, are illuminated. The therapist is given a greater understanding about what particular interventions will be comprehensible to the patient and why certain interventions may not be meeting with success. New directions for future goals, including possible vocational rehabilitation, also become clearer once the patient's level of intellectual ability is determined.

There are several other types of intelligence tests which may be employed to assess general level of IQ. While the WAIS–R is one of the most comprehensive, shorter versions of tests may be utilized to economize on time and finances. It should be noted, however, that shorter tests will also yield more limited information. The professional working with an addiction population must use clinical judgement in selecting the proper test to meet the patient's therapeutic needs. Trained professionals will be well versed in special considerations to be extended to elderly and culturally divergent populations when rendering IQ scores and estimates.

Halstead-Reitan Battery

This is a neuropsychological assessment tool designed to identify areas of possible neurological impairment and brain dysfunction likely in a population of chronic alcohol/drug abusers. This type of assessment requires a neuropsychologist who is especially trained in interpretation of the results. A neuropsychological evaluation is quite time-consuming and is, therefore, indicated only in situations where severe neurological damage is perceived or suspected.

Bender Visual-Motor Gestalt Test

This is a brief test which requires a patient to copy nine designs presented to him or her visually. The test is timed and the drawings are relatively simple in design. This instrument is designed as a screening device to detect possible organic brain dysfunction. Extremely poor performance on the Bender would indicate the need for further neurological and/or psychoneurological assessment but it is not a conclusive test alone.

Hooper Visual Organization Test

This is another test for organic factors. It consists of a series of pencil-sketched objects cut into several pieces. The patient is required to mentally and visually reorganize each percept into its proper form and then identify or name the object. Individuals with severe organic impairment will show marked deficiencies in this area.

Benton Visual Retention Test

This is another organic impairment testing tool which is a bit more extensive than the Bender. The test not only assesses grapho-motor abilities (the ability to actually draw the designs), but it focuses on memory function and whether or not the patient can retain information he/she has seen.

There are several other assessment tools available to explore human cognitive functioning, brain damage, memory deficits, and intelligence. It must be noted that the major reason for such assessment is to tailor the patient's therapeutic program to best meet their specific needs.

Projective Tests

House-Tree-Person Test

This is a tool devised to help a trained clinician determine aspects of personality style and offer a window into the inner world of the patient, their fantasies, wishes and areas of inadequacy. The drawings may also cue the possibility of organic impairment if the quality is notably poor and underdeveloped. Patients are similarly asked to draw pictures of a house, a tree, and then a person. They may then be directed to draw a figure of the opposite sex, upon completion of their first choice figure. Advanced artistic ability is neither expected or required, but rather, it is the placement of the figures and the content of the pictures rendered which will be analyzed.

The advantage of this test is that it requires very little time and can often be done in the initial evaluation phase, often during the first session. Although there are formalized scoring and interpretations available, an experienced clinician in testing will be able to glean much information from a brief review of the productions.

Thematic Apperception Test (TAT)

This projective test presents a card depicting a scene which conveys a certain level of ambiguous activity. The patient's task is to verbally relate a story with a beginning, middle, and ending that describes the nature of occurrences reflected in the picture. The open-ended, minimally-structured aspects of the test are designed to allow the patient to freely associate ideas throughout the test. The skilled clinician will be able to detect much information about the patient's view of the world and other people. Level of interpersonal abilities, defense mechanisms most often employed, and socialization skills are also revealed (Bellack, 1975).

Clinically, results of the TAT can assist to determine how well a patient will interact in a certain type of treatment testing. Conflicts with various images such as mother, father, or male/female peers are often revealed and may shed light on certain problems in group dynamics, etc. Abilities for conflict resolution and how the patient deals with stress and confrontation may also be revealed.

Rorschach Ink Blot Test

This test is comprised of ten standard ink blots which are shown to patients one at a time. The patient is then requested to "free associate" or verbalize whatever comes to mind as they study the blots. The test is semistructured in that the cards are always given in a certain order, but there are no directions given about what to say about the blots. There are several methods by which to score this test, all of which require extensive training. The scoring does yield some qualitative and quantitative data about the patient's responses, yet there are no right or wrong answers.

Results of the Rorschach can be very useful in the diagnosis of a thought disorder and psychotic process. The test taps unconscious levels of intrapsychic functioning, whereas the TAT deals more with material at the preconscious level. An individual with suspected psychotic features or borderline tendencies should be given a battery of these aforementioned projective tests administered by a qualified psychologist at some point in treatment.

Rotter Incomplete Sentences Blank

This is one of numerous incomplete sentence tests which provide the beginning of a sentence known as a sentence stem. The patient is then asked to complete the sentence in a way that is meaningful or true for them. This projective technique can be extremely flexible because sentences can be designed to pull information from any general area. The Rotter, however, is a more structured version and does provide an individual rating system which can assist in screening efforts. The Washington University Sentence Completion Test (WUSCT) by Loevinger, Wessler, & Redmore (1970) reflects the theoretical perspective of its author and yields a seven-stages scale that profiles the psychological/ego development of the patient (Anastasi, p. 571).

Word Association Tests

These are verbal techniques in which a selected list of words are presented and the testee is requested to respond with the first word that enters his/her mind. The words presented are usually presumed to have some psychological significance, often a psychosexual nature. The task is to unearth patterns or trends of psychosexual conflict in accordance with psychoanalytic theory. The interpretation of such tests is often vague and heavily dependent upon the assumed experience of the tester. While such tests are not essential parts of an assessment battery, they may prove useful to trained examiners who wish to obtain additional corroborating evidence for their projective interpretations.

SPECIAL TESTING CONCERNS

There are some special concerns in the substance abuse population regarding testing which are noteworthy. While the tests described thus far offer a well-rounded overall assessment of psychological and intellectual functioning, they do not address the specialized needs apparent in certain members of the substance abuse population. Such instances dictate that additional assessment may be warranted to ensure thorough rehabilitative services. A review of these special consideration will follow.

Education Tests

Some individuals may require assessment of their basic educational skills in order to properly determine a realistic vocational rehabilitation plan. Educational psychologists are well trained in such instruments that can help to determine the actual quantity and quality of a patient's present fund of knowledge while also offering information regarding the possibility of learning disabilities. This type of assessment can help to determine a patient's specific reading level, vocabulary abilities, etc. These skills are often critical to future job prospects and impact on the ability for the patient to comprehend written literature concerning recovery. Patients with an identified reading handicap can be given tapes and provided alternative modalities for receiving information regarding effective coping strategies in recovery. Specific tests for cognitive dysfunction and learning disabilities are also available.

Occupational Tests

Occupational therapy and testing is an area of assessment often used to chemically addicted individuals. These tests can assist in identifying particular areas of strength and weakness in relation to actual job-oriented skills. While these tests would not be part of an initial clinical evaluation or routine psychological battery, there may be times when patients can benefit from specific application of such testing might be in an individual who exhibits notable organic impairment and has demonstrated drastic declining performance on the job over a significant period of time.

Attitude, Interest, and Values Tests

These tools help to assess additional aspects of vocationally-related issues. The interest tests are extremely useful in determining the differences between skills a patient may excel at and those they have an actual interest to pursue based on an affinity to using such skills. It is not sufficient to be good at a particular skill, but rather, one must also reflect a strong personal interest in a certain job function. Attitude and value scales shed further light on a patient's level of socialization and prove useful for patients suspected of a personality disorder or antisocial tendencies. These factors can impact on the patient's progress in group and individual therapy; therefore, additional assessment in these areas is recommended to obtain a more specific profile on areas of deficient socialization skills, comprehensive, etc.

SEXUAL ABUSE VICTIMS

There is an ever-increasing awareness of the link between substance abuse and the incidence of sexual abuse in the dysfunctional family system. Many individuals who are addicted, and even some who are perpetrators of sexual and physical abuse themselves, may also be victims of the same type of assault in their own childhood. It is established that individuals who are exposed to high levels of repetitive trauma, violence, and physical/sexual assault in early childhood are prime candidates to develop dissociative disorders.

Dissociation is a natural process by which all people escape from the pressures of daily life and retreat to various levels of decreased awareness for momentary periods of time, such as when daydreaming. Dissociative disorders, however, manifest as extreme disturbances in the normal abilities to integrate behaviors, affect, sensation, and the knowledge of events or memory (BASK Model, Bennett Braun, 1986). There are several types of dissociative disorders presently specified in the DSM–III–R (Diagnostic and Statistical Manual of Mental Disorders-Revised, 1987). These are psychogenic amnesia, psychogenic fugue, depersonalization disorder, derealization disorder, multiple personality disorder, and dissociative disorder NOS. A full discussion of these disorders is beyond the scope of this chapter, other than to say that a consideration of possible dissociative symptoms in the substance abuse population is essential.

The most comprehensive assessment tool available to assist in the proper diagnosis of a dissociative disorder is the SCID–D (Structured Clinical Interview for DSM–III–R: Dissociative Disorders). This is an in-depth clinical interview developed by Marlene Steinberg, M.D. (1987) at Yale University which focuses on five major symptoms of dissociation including: (1) amnesia; (2) depersonalization; (3) derealization; (4) identity confusion; (5) identity alteration. The test yields a profile with severity ratings for each of the five symptoms to assist in treatment planning. It is also the most useful tool in the diagnosis of multiple personality disorder. Training is required for accurate administration and scoring of the SCID–D. It is recommended that patients in need of such assessment be referred to a specialist in the field of dissociation for examination and diagnosis.

There are other instruments which assess aspects of dissociation such as the Dissociative Experiences Scale (DES: Bernstein, E. & Putnam, F., 1986) and the DDIS (Ross, C., 1988). These questionnaires are quick to administer, require no specialized training, and are based solely on self-report. While these tests do serve as useful screening devices, the direct nature of the questions allows for easy distortion, denial, or inaccurate reporting by patients. In addition, some individuals may find questions particularly disturbing, whereas the SCID–D is more indirective and may therefore be less anxiety-provoking for those patients. The SCID–D focuses solely on symptoms rather than actual experiences of abuse, and offers an incisive yet gentle revelation of dissociative phenomenon experienced by patients.

This has been a general overview of the wide variety of testing tools available to the clinician assessing the needs of the prescription drug abuser, alcoholic, and addict. The effective clinical interviewer will gain at least some familiarity with these tests sufficient enough to be able to recommend or refer patients for these testing services when indicated. The proper and thorough assessment of the substance abuser is a prime factor in accurate and specifically tailored treatment planning essential to each patient caught in the life or death struggle we call addiction.

REFERENCES

Alcoholics Anonymous. (1976). New York: Alcoholics Anonymous World Services, Inc.

American Psychiatric Association. (1987). *Diagnostic and Statistical Manual of Mental Disorders* (3rd ed. rev.). Washington, DC: Multiple authors.

Anastasi, A. (1976). *Psychological testing* (4th ed.). New York: Macmillan.

Bellak, L. (1975). *The T.A.T., C.A.T. and the S.A.T. in clinical use* (3rd ed.). New York: Grune & Stratton.

Bernstein, E. & Putnam, F. (1986). Development, reliability and validity of a dissociation scale. *Journal of Nervous and Mental Disease, 174:* 727–735.

Boon, S., & Draijer, N. (1991). Diagnosing dissociative disorders in the Netherlands: A pilot study with The Structured Clinical Interview for DSM–III–R: Dissociative Disorders. *American Journal of Psychiatry, 148* (4): 458–462.

Bratter, T.E., & Forrest, G.G. (1985). *Alcoholism and substance abuse: Strategies for clinical intervention.* New York: The Free Press (division of Macmillan, Inc.).

Braun, B.G. (1990). Dissociative Disorders as sequelea to incest in incest-related syndromes of adult psychopathology. In R.P. Kluft (Ed.), *Childhood antecedents of multiple personality.* (pp. 227–246). Washington, DC: American Psychiatric Press.

Chappel, J. (July, 1986). *Handling User and Abuser Cases.* Lecture presented at the National Judicial College on Alcohol and Drugs: Princeton, New Jersey.

Ewing, J.A., & Rouse, B.A. (February, 1970). *Identifying the hidden alcoholic.* Paper presented at the 29th International Congress on Alcoholism and Drug Dependence, Sydney, Australia.

Goff, D.C., Olin, J.A., Jenike, M.A., et al. (1992). Dissociative symptoms in patients with obsessive-compulsive disorder. *Journal of Nervous and Mental Disease, 180* (5): 332–337.

Hester, R.K., & Miller, W.R. (1989). *Handbook of alcoholism treatment approaches: Effective alternatives.* New York: Pergamon Press.

Klopfer, B., & Davidson, H.H. (1962). *The Rorschach Technique: An introductory manual.* New York: Harcourt, Brace, and Jovanovich.

Kluft, R. (1985). *Childhood antecedents of multiple personality.* Washington, DC: American Psychiatric Press.

Matarazzo, J.D. (1972). *Wechsler's measurement and appraisal of adult intelligence* (5th ed.). New York: Oxford University Press.

Metzger, L. (1988). *From denial to recovery.* San Francisco/London: Jossey-Bass.

Nace, E.P. (1987). *The treatment of alcoholism.* New York: Brunner-Mazel.

Putnam, F.W. (1987). Dissociation as a response to extreme trauma. In R.P. Kluft (Ed.). *Childhood antecedents of multiple personality.* (pp. 65–97), Washington, DC, American Psychiatric Press.

Putnam, F.W. (1989). *Diagnosis and treatment of multiple personality disorder.* New York: The Guilford Press.

Riley, K. (1988). Measurement of dissociation. *Journal of Nervous and Mental Disease, 176:* 444–450.

Ross, C., Heber, S., Norton, G.R., et al. (1989). The Dissociative Disorders Interview Schedule: A structural interview. *Dissociation, 2* (3): 169–189.

Selzer, M.L. (1971). *The Alcoholisms: Detection, Assessment and Diagnosis.* New York: Human Sciences Press.

Steinberg, M. (1993). *The Structured Clinical Interview for DSM–IV–Dissociative Disorders,* Washington, DC: American Psychiatric Press.

Steinberg, M., Rounsaville, B., & Cicchetti, D.V. (1990). The Structured Clinical Interview for DSM–III–R. Dissociative Disorders: Preliminary report on a new diagnostic instrument. *American Journal of Psychiatry, 147:* 76–82.

Stern, E.M. (1985). *Psychotherapy and the religiously committed patient.* New York: The Haworth Press.

Yalom, I.D. (1980). *Existential Psychotherapy.* New York: Basic Books.

Chapter 7

PRESCRIPTION DRUG ABUSE AND DEPENDENCE, ANXIETY, AND MOOD DISORDERS: *INTERACTIONS AND IMPLICATIONS*

Jeffrey S. Kahn

INTRODUCTION

Substance abuse and mental disorders take an enormous toll on their victims, their families, and society in general. In any six-month period, 30 million Americans suffer from alcohol, other drug, or mental disorders. Direct health care costs from these disorders total 50.3 billion dollars, and when indirect costs such as productivity loss and property damage are added in, the total approaches 218 billion dollars per year, and that does not include the doubled use of general health care resources by this group. The most final and irreversible cost is the significant mortality caused by these disorders. Between suicide, accidental overdoses, and substance use-related accidents and homicides, over 108,000 deaths per year result. The cost in "potentially productive years of life lost" is disproportionately high, for the victims are often young people (Kamerow, Pincus, & Macdonald, 1986). The risk of suicide in alcoholics is estimated to be 30 times greater than that of the population as a whole (Frances & Allen, 1991) and 19 percent of drug abusers make suicide attempts (Saxon, cited in Frances & Allen, 1991).

The problems of alcohol abuse/dependence, other drug abuse/dependence (including prescription drug abuse and dependence), and mental/psychological disorders (including anxiety and mood disorders), interact in complex, varied, and not fully understood ways. They are frequently unrecognized and untreated, despite the fact that in many cases, treatment can provide effective help and avoid exacerbation or complications of the disorders.

Prescription drug abuse and dependence (PDAD) is one form of substance abuse, often very similar to other forms and often occurring simultaneously with them. Prescription drug abusers are diverse and their characteristics have considerable overlap with the population of illicit drug abusers and alcohol abusers. Moreover, the effects of the drugs are often the same (Greenfield, 1994). However, there are some differences in some cases in the drugs and the abusers. In addition to the standard classes of drugs abused by illicit drug abusers (hallucinogens, stimulants, narcotic analgesics, and depressants), there are additional prescription drugs that are sometimes abused: "unexpected prescription drug abuse agents" including beta-adrenergic blockers, analgesics, and antitussives, and dangerous noncontrolled drugs such as antidepressants, anorexiants, and cold remedies (Weiss & Greenfield, 1986).

Mellinger, Balter, Manheimer, Cisin, and Perry (1978), in their study of psychic distress, life crisis, and use of psychotherapeutic medication, found a relationship between degree of life crisis and level of psychic distress. Psychotherapeutic drug use (including major or minor tranquilizers, daytime sedatives, and antidepressants) was clearly and strongly related to the degree of psychic distress. Frequency of psychotherapeutic drug used was highest among those reporting high levels of both anxiety and depression. It can be assumed that a portion of the psychotherapeutic drug use (which was largely comprised of benzodiazepine use) constituted PDAD or could evolve into it.

Based on demographic differences in both the levels of distress and the methods of coping with distress found in this study, it may be expected that a higher representation of women than men and older rather than younger people would be prescription drug users and abusers. The authors note that males and younger people tend to use moderate-to-heavy alcohol consumption as an alternative to psychotherapeutic drug use as a way of coping with psychic distress and life crisis.

Carlin and Strauss (cited in Leigh, 1985) categorized drug users into three groups: basic self-medicators, street-wise self-medicators, and streetwise recreational users. The basic self-medicators had more depressive symptoms than the other groups and obtained their drugs through prescriptions. The streetwise self-medicators were more psychologically disordered than the streetwise recreational users, but both of the latter groups obtained their drugs illicitly.

While the focus of this chapter is on mood and anxiety disorders as they interact with PDAD, it is important to note the numerous other mental disorders which frequently coexist and interact with PDAD. The Somatoform Disorders are characterized by the presence of physical symptoms for which there is no organic basis. Included in this category are Hypochondriasis, Somatization Disorder, in which one experiences many uncomfortable "physical" symptoms, and Somatoform Pain Disorder, all of which are logical precursors of PDAD, as are physical conditions which result in organically caused pain. Analgesics, including opiates, would be high probability drugs of abuse. Sleep Disorders are also logical precursors of prescription drug use and possible subsequent abuse. Sedatives for Insomnia or stimulants for Hypersomnia are likely drugs of abuse. Eating Disorders are associated, in some cases diagnostically, with abuse of anorexiants (diet pills), both prescription and nonprescription, laxatives, and diuretics. Attention Deficit Hyperactivity Disorder (ADHD), formerly termed Attention Deficit Disorder or minimal brain dysfunction, is itself associated with high rates of Oppositional Defiant Disorder and Conduct Disorder. Conduct Disorder, if uncorrected, can become Antisocial Personality Disorder in older adolescents and adults. The disregard for social norms and lawful behavior associated with the latter disorders are frequently associated with substance abuse/dependence of all kinds, and the paradoxical calming effect of stimulants on ADHD, when accidentally discovered, can be self-administered in the form of cocaine or illicitly obtained amphetamines. Another personality disorder frequently associated with substance abuse is Borderline Personality Disorder. Schizophrenia in its various forms frequently coexists with substance abuse, particularly in "Young Adult Chronic Psychiatric Patients," who, along with other more severely mentally disordered individuals, comprise the population termed "mentally ill chemical abusers" or MICA's. Of the mood and anxiety disorders, individuals with Bipolar Disorder are the most likely to be included in this group, mania is often misdiagnosed as schizophrenia (Pope, 1979).

While the preceding categories of mental disorders, in addition to mood and anxiety disorders, are most likely to be comorbid with PDAD, any mental disorder causing distress and discomfort may be a trigger for the search for pharmaceutical relief, either directly, or by causing symptoms of anxiety and depression. Matuschka (1985, p. 49), expressing the self-medication view of the relationship between psychiatric disorders and substance abuse, states unequivocally that "The basic element of abuse is some psychological instability for which chemical substances may represent the so-called 'therapeutic agent' needed for self-treatment." Other possible mental disorders which could lead to substance abuse include Organic Mental Disorders, Dissociative Disorders, Bereavement, and Adjustment Disorders. Finally, it should be remembered that in an undetermined percentage of cases, a substance use disorder may precede and/or cause the mental disorder, and not follow or result from it.

Just as with more common forms of substance abuse, there are "pure" cases of PDAD without any additional diagnosable condition which is listed in the Diagnostic and Statistical Manual of Mental Disorders (DSM–III–R) (American Psychiatric Association [APA], 1987). However, given the high comorbidity of substance abuse and other psychiatric diagnoses, they are probably a minority. While 18 percent of the population will have a substance use disorder of some kind in their lives, two thirds of the substance abusers will have an additional psychiatric disorder (Robbins, Helzer, Weissman et al., cited in Frances & Allen, 1991).

Since this chapter is devoted to an examination of PDAD in people with coexisting anxiety and mood disorders, the focus will be on "dual diagnosis" cases. The term "dual diagnosis" in the field of substance abuse refers to cases in which there exists both a diagnosable psychiatric disorder and a substance use disorder. (It should be noted that some substance abuse professionals restrict the use of the term "dual diagnosis" to cases in which there is a substance use disorder and a particularly severe psychiatric disorder such as schizophrenia or bipolar disorder.)

DSM-IV DIAGNOSIS: AN OVERVIEW

In order to clarify the relationship of multiple psychiatric and substance use disorders, a brief overview of the DSM–IV structure is presented below. In the revised edition of the DSM–IV, a multiaxial system is used to give more recognition to the interactions of developmental disorders, personality disorders, physical disorders, life stresses, and level of functioning with clinical syndromes (see Table 7-1). A complete DSM–IV diagnosis includes all five axes.

A list of major diagnostic categories for Axis I is given in Table 7-2. A list of the developmental and personality disorders which constitute Axis II is given in Table 7-3.

It is important to note that more than one diagnosis can be made on Axis I, II, and III. It is also possible that an individual may have no diagnosis on Axis I, II, or III. However, the population addressed in this chapter, by definition, has at least two Axis I diagnoses: a Psychoactive Substance Use Disorder and a Mood or Anxiety Disorder. These two

Table 7-1. Multiaxial Diagnostic System (*after DSM–IV, 1994*).

Axis I	Clinical Disorders Other Conditions That May Be a Focus of Clinical Attention
Axis II	Personality Disorders Mental Retardation
Axis III	General Medical Conditions
Axis IV	Psychological and Environmental Problems
Axis V	Global Assessment of Functioning

Table 7-2. Axis I Categories (*after DSM–IV, 1994*).

Disorders Usually First Diagnosed in Infancy, Childhood, or Adolescence

Delirium, Dementia, Anbestic, and Other Cognitive Disorders

Mental Disorders Due to a General Medical Condition Not Elsewhere Classified

Substance-Related Disorders

Schizophrenia and Other Psychotic Disorders

Mood Disorders

Anxiety Disorders

Somatoform Disorders

Factitious Disorders

Dissociative Disorders

Sexual and Gender Identity Disorders

Eating Disorders

Sleep Disorders

Impulsive-Control Disorders Not Elsewhere Classified

Adjustment Disorders

Other Conditions That May Be a Focus of Clinical Attention

Additional Codes

categories of Axis I diagnoses will be examined in more detail in order to clarify the diagnostic system and to facilitate an understanding of the possible interactions between them.

Table 7-3. Axis II Categories (*after DSM–IV, 1994*).

Disorders Usually First Diagnosed in Infancy, Childhood, or Adolescence

Mental Retardation
Personality Disorder
  Cluster A
    Paranoid
    Schizoid
    Schizotypal
  Cluster B
    Antisocial
    Borderline
    Histrionic
    Narcissistic
  Cluster C
    Avoidant
    Dependent
    Obsessive-Compulsive
    Personality Disorder Not Otherwise Specified (NOS)

DSM–IV DIAGNOSIS:
PSYCHOACTIVE SUBSTANCE USE DISORDERS

Psychoactive Substance Use Disorders describe "the symptoms and maladaptive behavioral changes associated with more or less regular use of psychoactive substances that affect the central nervous system" (APA, 1987). They are conceptualized as mental disorders and distinguished from nonpathological psychoactive substance use such as moderate drinking or taking medication as prescribed. They are also to be distinguished from the category of Psychoactive Substance-Induced Organic Mental Disorders, in that the latter category refers to the "direct acute or chronic effects of such substances on the central nervous system," including intoxication, withdrawal, delirium, withdrawal delirium, delusional disorder, mood disorder, and other syndromes (APA, 1987). The psychoactive substances potentially causing organic mental disorders are alcohol, amphetamine and related substances, caffeine, cannabis, cocaine, hallucinogen, inhalant, nicotine, opioid, phencyclidine (PCP) and related substances, and sedative, hypnotic, or anxiolytic. These are the same substances which are listed under Psychoactive Substance Use Disorders, with the exception of caffeine, which is not included as a substance of abuse or dependence.

In the category of Psychoactive Substance Use Disorders, the criteria for "Dependence" and for the residual diagnosis of "Abuse" are the same for all substances. For a diagnosis of "Dependence," a person must have at least three of the nine symptoms listed in Table 7-4 and some of the symptoms must have persisted for at least one month or occurred repeatedly over a longer period (APA, 1987). Criteria are also given for rating the severity of the dependence as "mild," "moderate," or "severe," as well as for conditions "In Partial Remission" or "In Full Remission."

Table 7-4. Diagnostic Criteria for Substance Dependence (*after DSM–IV, 1994*).

A maladaptive pattern of substance use, leading to clinically significant impairment or distress, as manifested by three (or more) of the following, occurring at any time in the same 12-month period:

   (1) tolerance, as defined by either of the following:
      (a) a need for markedly increased amounts of the substance to achieve intoxication or desired effect
      (b) markedly diminished effect with continued use of the same amount of the substance
   (2) withdrawal, as manifested by either of the following:
      (a) the characteristic withdrawal syndrome for the substance (refer to Criteria A and B of the criteria sets for Withdrawal from the specific substances)
      (b) the same (or a closely related) substance is taken to relieve or avoid withdrawal symptoms
   (3) the substance is often taken in larger amounts or over a longer period than was intended
   (4) there is a persistent desire or unsuccessful efforts to cut down or control substance use
   (5) a great deal of time is spent in activities necessary to obtain the substance (e.g., chain-smoking), or recover from its effects
   (6) important social, occupational, or recreational activities are given up or reduced because of substance use
   (7) the substance use is continued despite knowledge of having a persistent or recurrent physical or psychological problem that is likely to have been caused or exacerbated by the substance (e.g., current cocaine use despite recognition of cocaine-induced depression, or continued drinking despite recognition that an ulcer was made worse by alcohol consumption)

Specify with or without physiologic dependence
Note course specifiers

For the residual diagnosis of "Abuse," a person must never have met the criteria for "Dependence" on the particular substance, but still manifest a maladaptive pattern of use which has persisted for at least one month, or which has occurred repeatedly over a longer period. The maladaptive pattern of psychoactive substance use must be indicated by at least one of the following: "(1) continued use despite knowledge of having a persistent or recurrent social, occupational, psychological, or physical problem that is caused or exacerbated by use of the psychoactive substance; (2) recurrent use in situations in which use is physically hazardous (e.g., driving while intoxicated)" (APA, 1987).

In the DSM–IV system, a separate diagnosis is made for every psychoactive substance which is used in such a way as to meet the criteria for either dependence or abuse. Therefore, it is possible for an individual to be diagnosed as dependent on several substances and abusive of others. However, an individual is never diagnosed as dependent and abusing the same substance. The diagnosis of Polysubstance Dependence is used when an individual has used at least three types of psychoactive substances (not counting nicotine or caffeine) for at least six months, no single substance has predominated, the criteria for dependence has been met for the group of substances, but not for any single one. The diagnoses of Psychoactive Substance Dependence/Abuse Not Otherwise Specified are used when there is dependence or abuse of a psychoactive substance which cannot be classified as one of the aforementioned class of chemicals or as an initial diagnosis in cases of dependence or abuse in which the specific substance is not yet known (APA, 1987).

DSM–IV DIAGNOSIS: MOOD DISORDERS

This group of disorders has as its essential characteristic a disturbance of mood. Mood is defined as "a prolonged emotion that colors the whole psychic life" (APA, 1987). The mood generally is characterized by depression or elation as part of a full or partial Manic or Depressive Syndrome and is not caused by any other physical or mental disorder. A mood syndrome consisting of a predominant depressed or manic mood, lasting at least two weeks and accompanied by other symptoms described below, could be part of a Mood Disorder or part of nonmood disorders. A mood episode is a mood syndrome which is not attributable to physical cause or another mental disorder other than a mood disorder. A mood disorder is determined by the pattern of mood episodes. For example, Major Depression is characterized by at least one Major Depressive Episode and no present or past Manic Episodes; Bipolar Disorders would require the presence of a current mood episode; if the current episode is depressed, there must have been a prior manic episode to make the diagnosis of

Bipolar Disorder. The diagnostic criteria for Manic Episode are presented in Table 7-5. The diagnostic criteria for Major Depressive Episode are given in Table 7-6 (APA, 1987).

Table 7-5. Diagnostic Criteria for Manic Episode (*after DSM-IV, 1994*).

A. A distinct period of abnormally and persistently elevated, expansive, or irritable mood, lasting at least 1 week (or any duration if hospitalization is necessary).
B. During the period of mood disturbance, three (or more) of the following symptoms have persisted (four if the mood is only irritable) and have been presented to a significant degree:
   (1) inflated self esteem or grandiosity
   (2) decreased need for sleep (e.g., feels rested after only 3 hours of sleep)
   (3) more talkative than usual or pressure to keep talking
   (4) flight of ideas or subjective experience that thoughts are racing
   (5) distractibility (i.e., attention too easily drawn to unimportant or irrelevant external stimuli)
   (6) increase in goal-directed activity (either socially, at work or school, or sexually) or psychomotor agitation
   (7) excessive involvement in pleasurable activities that have a high potential for painful consequences (e.g., engaging in unrestrained buying sprees, sexual indiscretions, or foolish business investments)
C. The symptoms do not meet criteria for a Mixed Episode.
D. The mood disturbance is sufficiently severe to cause marked impairment in occupational functioning or in usual social activities or relationships with others, or to necessitate hospitalization to prevent harm to self or others, or there are psychotic features.
E. The symptoms are not due to the direct physiological effects of a substance (e.g., a drug of abuse, a medication, or other treatment) or a general medical condition (e.g., hyperthyroidism).

Bipolar Disorders include Mixed, Manic, and Depressed types, as well as Cyclothymia, which some believe to be a less severe form of Bipolar Disorder. In Bipolar Disorder, Mixed, there are symptoms of both Major Depressive and Manic Episodes either simultaneously or alternating every few days. In Bipolar Disorder, Manic, the person is currently in a Manic Episode; there need not have been a history of prior mood episodes. In Bipolar Disorder, Depressed, the person is currently in a Major Depressive Episode and has a history of at least one Manic Episode. In Cyclothymia, there is a chronic mood disturbance (two years minimum for adults, one year for children and adolescents), characterized by several hypomanic and depressed periods and without

Table 7-6. Diagnostic Criteria for Major Depressive Episode (*after DSM-IV, 1994*).

(A) Five (or more) of the following symptoms have been present during the same 2-week period and represent a change from previous functioning; at least one of the following symptoms is either (1) depressed mood or (2) loss of interest or pleasure.

Note: Do not include symptoms that are clearly due to a general medical condition, or mood-incongruent delusions or hallucinations.

  (1) depressed mood most of the day, nearly every day, as indicated by either subjective report (e.g., feels sad or empty) or observation made by others (e.g., appears tearful). **Note:** In children and adolescents, can be irritable mood.
  (2) markedly diminished interest or pleasure in all, or almost all, activities most of the day, nearly every day (as indicated by either subjective account or observation made by others)
  (3) significant weight loss when not dieting or weight gain (e.g., a change of more than 5% of body weight in a month), or decrease or increase in appetite nearly every day. **Note:** In children, consider failure to make expected weight gains.
  (4) insomnia or hypersomnia nearly every day
  (5) psychomotor agitation or retardation nearly every day (observable by others, not merely subjective feelings of restlessness or being slowed down)
  (6) fatigue or loss of energy nearly every day
  (7) feelings of worthlessness or excessive or inappropriate guilt (which may be delusional) nearly every day (not merely self-reproach or guilt about being sick)
  (8) diminished ability to think or concentrate, or indecisiveness, nearly every day (either by subjective account or as observed by others)
  (9) recurrent thoughts of death (not just fear of dying), recurrent suicidal ideation without a specific plan, or a suicide attempt or a specific plan for committing suicide

(B) The symptoms do not meet criteria for a mixed Episode.
(C) the symptoms cause clinically significant distress or impairment in social, occupational, or other important areas of functioning.
(D) The symptoms are not due to the direct physiological effects of a substance (e.g., a drug of abuse, a medication) or a general medical condition (e.g., hypothyroidism).
(E) The symptoms are not better accounted for by Bereavement, i.e., after the loss of a loved one, the symptoms persist for longer than 2 months or are characterized by marked functional impairment, morbid preoccupation with worthlessness, suicidal ideation, psychotic symptoms, or psychomotor retardation.

periods free of these moods lasting longer than two months. Hypomanic Episodes differ from Manic Episodes in that the mood disturbance is not severe enough to require hospitalization or cause obvious impairment in social or vocational functioning. In Cyclothymia, the depressed periods are not severe enough to meet the criteria for Major Depressive Episode. The most common complication of a Manic episode is Psychoactive Substance Abuse and in Cyclothymia, "Psychoactive Substance Abuse is common as a result of self-treatment with sedatives and alcohol during the depressed periods and the self-indulgent use of stimulants and psychedelic substances during the hypomanic periods" (APA, 1987).

Depressive Disorders include Major Depression, Single Episode and Recurrent, Dysthymia, and Depressive Disorder, Not Otherwise specified. The diagnosis or Major Depression requires the presence of a Major Depressive Episode (and a history of prior episodes for Recurrent type) and no history of a Manic or "unequivocal" hypomanic Episode.

Dysthymia is a less severe and more chronic form of depression that is defined similarly to Cyclothymia except that there are only depressed periods (not severe enough to meet the criteria for Major Depressive Episode) and no hypomanic periods. The criteria for Dysthymia, during the depressed periods, are at least two of the following: poor appetite or overeating, insomnia or hypersomnia, low energy or fatigue, low self-esteem, poor concentration or difficulty making decisions, and feelings of hopelessness. While the complications of Dysthymia are similar to those of Major Depression, there is a greater likelihood of developing substance abuse or dependence because of the chronicity of the disorder (APA, 1987). It is possible to have a Major Depression superimposed on Dysthymia. This is sometimes termed "double depression."

The final mood disorder is the residual category of Depressive Disorder, Not Otherwise Specified, for disorders with depressive characteristics that do not meet the criteria for any specific Mood Disorder (APA, 1987).

DSM-IV DIAGNOSIS: ANXIETY DISORDERS

The predominant features of this class of disorders, which are given the alternative name of anxiety and phobic neuroses, are symptoms of anxiety and avoidance behavior. The disorders included in this group include: Panic Disorder, with and without Agoraphobia, Agoraphobia without History of Panic Disorder, Social Phobia, Simple Phobia, Obsessive Compulsive Disorder, Posttraumatic Stress Disorder, Generalized

Anxiety Disorder, and Anxiety Disorder Not Otherwise Specified. These disorders, as a group, are the most frequently found psychiatric disorders in the general population, and the victims of these disorders are at particular risk for episodic, abusive, or dependent usage of alcohol, barbiturates or anxiolytics (APA, 1987).

In panic disorders, the essential features are recurrent periods of intense fear or discomfort, not caused by exposure to a specific feared stimulus as in a Simple Phobia such as Claustrophobia, or by being the focus of attention as in Social Phobia. The majority of cases develop symptoms of Agoraphobia, the fear of being in places where escape might be difficult or embarrassing if a panic attack occurred. Avoidance of these situations can develop to a point where a person can become totally homebound in severe cases. There are 13 symptoms which are sometimes experienced in panic attacks, at least four of which must be experienced to constitute a full panic attack; with fewer than four symptoms, they are termed limited symptom attacks. Psychoactive Substance Use Disorders can be a complication of Panic Disorders, particularly alcohol and anxiolytics (APA, 1987). Table 7-7 lists the panic attack symptoms.

Table 7-7. Panic Attack Symptoms (*after DSM–IV, 1994*).

A discrete period of intense fear or discomfort, in which four (or more) of the following symptoms developed abruptly and reached a peak within 10 minutes:
   (1) palpitations, pounding heart, or accelerated heart rate
   (2) sweating
   (3) trembling or shaking
   (4) sensations of shortness of breath or smothering
   (5) feeling of choking
   (6) chest pain or discomfort
   (7) nausea or abdominal distress
   (8) feeling dizzy, unsteady, lightheaded, or faint
   (9) derealization (feeling of unreality) or depersonalization (being detached from oneself)
  (10) fear of losing control or going crazy
  (11) fear of dying
  (12) paresthesias (numbness or tingling sensations)
  (13) chills or hot flushes

Social Phobia has as its essential feature the fear of scrutiny by others while acting in a way that is humiliating, such as being unable to speak properly, choking on food, having trembling hands while writing, or being unable to urinate in a public lavatory. Exposure to the socially phobic situation(s) produces immediate anxiety, the phobic situations are avoided, and the avoidant behavior impedes social, occupational, or interpersonal functioning. The socially phobic person is aware that the fear is excessive. Episodic abuse of alcohol, barbiturates, and anxiolytics is a complication that people with this disorder are prone to (APA, 1987).

Similarly, in Simple Phobia, the fear is of a particular object or situation other than having a panic attack or the social situations defined in Social Phobia. There is avoidance of the phobic stimulus or it is endured with great anxiety and the person knows the fear is unreasonable. It is only diagnosed when the avoidant behavior impedes normal routines, relationships, and social activities, or when having the phobia causes significant distress.

Obsessive Compulsive Disorder (OCD) has, as its principal aspect, recurrent obsessions or compulsions which are of such an extent that they cause considerable distress to the individual and interfere with normal functioning. Obsessions are defined as "persistent ideas, thoughts, impulses, or images that are experienced, at least initially, as intrusive or senseless." Compulsions are "repetitive purposeful, and intentional behaviors that are performed in response to an obsession, according to certain rules, or in a stereotyped fashion" (APA, 1987). An example is an obsessive thought of being unclean and a resulting compulsion to wash one's hands. The person recognizes that the obsessions are his or her own thoughts (unlike in some psychotic conditions) and that the compulsive behaviors are extreme or unreasonable, but cannot be resisted because of the increasing anxiety that results. Abuse of alcohol and anxiolytics and Major Depression can be complications of OCD (APA, 1987).

Posttraumatic Stress Disorder is grouped with the anxiety disorders even though its key feature is the reexperiencing of the traumatic event and not anxiety or avoidance behavior. However, anxiety and avoidance of situations resembling the trauma are common and increased arousal is present. As the name suggests, this disorder results from the experience of an overwhelming event producing great fear or injury. The archetypal example of this disorder is produced in war experiences and was called "shell shock" in World War I and "battle fatigue" in World War II. Of course, traumatic stimuli could occur also through crime, accident, or natural disaster. Psychoactive Substance Use Disorders are "common complications" (APA, 1987).

Generalized Anxiety Disorder is characterized by unrealistic or excessive anxiety or worry about more than one situation lasting more than six months, during which symptoms are present more days than not. At least six of the eighteen symptoms shown in Table 7-8 are often present during anxiety states (APA, 1987).

Table 7-8. Symptom Criteria for Generalized Anxiety Disorder
(*after DSM-III-R, 1987; DSM-IV, 1994*).

The following categories of types of symptoms and symptoms themselves may be present when anxious.

MOTOR TENSION
1. trembling, twitching, or feeling shaky
2. muscle tension, aches, or soreness
3. restlessness
4. easy fatigability

AUTONOMIC HYPERACTIVITY
5. shortness of breath or smothering sensations
6. palpitations or accelerated heart rate (tachycardia)
7. sweating, or cold clammy hands
8. dry mouth
9. dizziness or lightheadedness
10. nausea, diarrhea, or other abdominal distress
11. flushes (hot flashes) or chills
12. frequent urination
13. trouble swallowing or "lump in throat"

VIGILANCE AND SCANNING
14. feeling keyed up or on edge
15. exaggerated startle response
16. difficulty concentrating or "mind going blank" because of anxiety
17. trouble falling or staying asleep
18. irritability

The final, residual diagnostic category is Anxiety Disorder Not Otherwise Specified, in which there are significant manifestations of anxiety and fearful avoidance, but the criteria for the other anxiety disorders are not met.

The DSM–IV lists Psychoactive Substance Use Disorders as complications for some but not all of the mood and anxiety disorders because there is not adequate documentation and frequency to make the generalization in every disorder. This does not imply that the other disorders do not raise the likelihood of substance abuse as well.

ETIOLOGY OF PSYCHOACTIVE SUBSTANCE USE DISORDERS

In her study of the etiology of substance abuse, Leigh (1985) states that "At present no single theory or model can adequately account for either the development or the maintenance of this problem." Although many investigators believe that certain mental disorders produce a proclivity to abuse certain substances, others maintain that the abuse of substances in fact leads to the mental disorders. In other words, comorbidity does not establish the causal directionality. Acknowledging the incompleteness of present understanding, much research has been done which demonstrates the impact of a wide variety of factors. Leigh (1985) proposes five categories of factors influencing substance abuse: biological, including biochemical, genetic, and physiological; cultural, including customs, mores, attitudes and social policy; environmental, including conditioning, learning, and life events; interpersonal, including social and familial; and intrapersonal, including developmental, personality, affect and cognition, and sex differences.

The cultural attitudes of the society toward drinking or other drug use determines its status in the hierarchy of social behavior, and customs and mores set the tone and feeling about use of different types of substances. While influencing consumption levels on the societal level, cultural attitudes do not explain abuse on an individual level.

Conditioning is the learning principle that behavior which produces a positive reward will increase in frequency. Animal studies show that cocaine is so reinforcing that rats, given an unlimited supply, will self-20 administer until they die. Other drugs produce other patterns in animals: some, like alcohol must first be established by conditioning and then will be used steadily. Others, such as hallucinogens, will not be increased by self-administration, even after conditioning. In addition to the reward of a pleasurable experience, rats can learn that alcohol or a sedative can help cope with the unpleasant experience of being shocked (Mello & Mendelson, cited in Leigh, 1985), a finding with implications for the self-medication hypothesis of substance abuse, discussed later. The learning principle of modeling can also account for some substance use:

adolescents with smoking parents are more likely to smoke themselves (Ahlgren, Norem, Hochhauser, & Garvin, cited in Leigh, 1985).

In the area of familial factors, there is some evidence for a genetic component, at least for the drug alcohol, but, as Cotton (cited in Leigh, 1985) reports, only 30 percent of people with alcohol problems have an alcoholic parent. Leigh (1985) concludes that the larger number of alcoholics from alcoholic families are due to environmental and social factors.

Intrapersonal factors concern individual differences and may be more relevant to the development of substance use in a particular person. Birth order and child rearing practices may contribute to dependency conflict and oral fixation (Leigh, 1985).

There is a clear disagreement between researchers who view such personal attributes as impulsivity, poor self-esteem, low ego strength, and low social conformity as precursors of substance abuse (Barnes, cited in Leigh, 1985) and those, like Vaillant (cited in Leigh, 1985), who view depression and antisocial personality as results of alcoholism (and, presumably, other drug dependence). Leigh (1985) concludes that there is no clear evidence for an alcoholic or drug-abusing personality as such; however, there may be subtypes.

Metzger (1988) also confronts the contradiction between studies which report certain personality traits in alcoholics repeatedly and consider them causative of alcoholism, and others which view them as consequences. He cites Catanzaro, who reports a list of personality traits which appear repeatedly in the literature. They include "a high level of anxiety in interpersonal relations, emotional immaturity, ambivalence toward authority, low tolerance for frustration, grandiosity, low self-esteem, feelings of isolation, perfectionism, guilt, compulsiveness, angry over-dependency, sex-role confusion, and inability to express angry feelings adequately." He also cites Bean, whose view is that the personality dysfunction is caused by the alcoholism, and Vaillant, who found that personality factors were secondary in determining who became alcoholic. The three variables most predictive of alcoholism were "ethnic membership and training, adolescent behavioral problems, and a family history of alcoholism." Metzger's (1988) own opinion is that "the personality structure of the alcoholic is not more flawed than that of nonalcoholics in the general public," and that, after a year of abstinence, alcoholics can function as well or better than average.

In thinking about the interaction of personality and substance abuse, it is useful to distinguish between personality traits and personality disorders. The DSM–IV defines personality traits as "enduring patterns of perceiving, relating to, and thinking about the environment and oneself." Personality disorders exist only when the personality traits are "inflexible and maladaptive and cause either significant functional impairment or subjective distress" (APA, 1987). Personality disorders are usually evident by adolescence or early adulthood and often precede any psychoactive substance use disorder. In such cases, and when the incidence of substance use is significantly higher than in individuals without diagnosable personality disorders, it is reasonable to assume that the preceding personality disorder is a predisposing factor to substance abuse. Mere personality traits may not be significantly influential. The DSM–IV states that for Antisocial Personality Disorder, "Psychoactive Substance Use Disorders are commonly associated diagnoses," Psychoactive Substance Abuse is a complication of Borderline Personality Disorder, and Alcohol Abuse or Dependence is a complication of Passive Aggressive Personality Disorder (APA, 1987). Frances & Allen (1991), in reviewing the literature, conclude that while no single personality disorder or group of traits is specific for addiction, addictive disorder may be "over-represented" in a number of personality disorders, including antisocial, borderline, narcissistic, dependent, and passive aggressive.

Leigh's (1985) review of studies dealing with the influence of affect on psychoactive substance use has particular significance for the self-medication hypothesis, for mood and possibly anxiety disorders as well. She cites studies as old as Rado's work which suggested that drugs are used to relieve depression, and Conger and Cappell and Herman who debated whether alcohol was a tension reducer. Also cited was Farber, Khavari, and Douglass' study which found that, among heavy drinkers, 93 percent described themselves as "escape" drinkers, seeking relief from negative affect rather than as social drinkers seeking positive feelings.

McLellan, Woody, and O'Brien (1979) studied the origin of specific psychiatric disorders in abusers of different drugs. Three groups of drug abusers (stimulant users, depressant users, and opiate users) who were admitted to a Veterans Hospital for drug abuse treatment at least once a year for six consecutive years were given psychiatric assessments at each admission. Initially, all groups had low symptom levels and there were no statistically significant differences between the groups. By the end of six years, five of the eleven stimulant users had developed psychoses and eight of the fourteen depressant users had developed serious depression, while the opiate users showed no change in psychopathology.

The authors offered two possible explanations for the increase in psychological symptoms in the first two groups. The first, which they label the "medication" theory (elsewhere termed "self-medication"), was that the symptoms underlying the disorders detected at the end of the six years were present at the beginning, but below the threshold for detection. If this were true, they may have influenced selection of drugs and pattern of use as a source of relief. This would account for the well known tendency of drug abusers to select chemicals with similar effects and reject other available types of drugs, and suggests use to enduce a specific effect. The second possible explanation, the "developmental" view, is that prolonged abuse of the specific types of drugs had a direct role in the origin and manifestation disorder, possibly through state-dependent learning or alterations in the biochemistry of the nervous system.

While a detailed discussion of nervous system biochemistry is beyond the scope of this chapter, a basic understanding of neurotransmitter theory is very helpful in grasping the psychopharmacology of licit and illicit drugs. Essentially, neurotransmitters are a group of naturally occurring brain/nervous system chemicals which allow communication between the nerve cells. Collectively, they influence all thinking, feeling, and behavior. Too much or too little of one or more of them can distort, exaggerate, or suppress normal cognition and emotion.

McLellan and Druley (1977), in their study of relationships between drugs of abuse and psychiatric diagnosis, found that abuse of amphetamine or hallucinogens was associated with paranoid schizophrenia and not depression, whereas abuse of barbiturates was associated with depression and not schizophrenia. While they point out that their data is only correlational and therefore not determining causality, they state that their findings are consistent with the monoamine balance theory of mental disorder. In its most accepted version, the theory suggests that too little of the central nervous system neurotransmitters dopamine and norepinephrine or too much of the neurotransmitter seratonin are correlated with clinical depression. Conversely, too much dopamine and epinephrine or too little seratonin are correlated with mania, hyperactivity, and possibly schizophrenia. The monoamine theory would predict specific mental disorders for individuals who have altered their monoamine balance through prolonged drug abuse. Since hallucinogens and amphetamines produce more dopamine and epinephrine and seratonin as well as sensitizing nerves to them, the theory would predict mania or schizophrenia, not depression. Conversely, barbiturates and sedative hypnotics reduce the functional availability of these central nervous system neurotransmitters and prolonged abuse would logically predict depression.

The hypothesis that addicts or alcoholics have lowered levels of neurotransmitters and self-administer their mood altering chemicals to raise the levels has been called the reserpine hypothesis by Goodwin (cited in Frances & Allen, 1991). In fact, at first, levels do increase, but then levels fall off even more, which may spur increased drinking. Experimental intoxication studies show that chronic intoxication regularly leads to deterioration of mood and depressive syndromes which are often coupled with suicidal thoughts. The same process may occur with cocaine (Frances and Allen, 1991).

An additional explanation of the self-medication phenomenon is offered by Milkman and Frosch (1973), who explored the preferential use of heroin and amphetamine and its relationship to personality. First, they determined that 75 percent of their subjects stated a specific preference for either heroin or amphetamine and had a long involvement with only one, although all had experienced both drugs. This finding was in accordance with that of McLellan & Druley (1977), who found that less than 5 percent of their drug abusing sample abused drugs with different pharmacological actions. In other words, while abuse of combinations of drugs with similar pharmacological actions like heroin and barbiturates was common, abuse of combinations like amphetamines and barbiturates was rare. This finding is supportive of a fundamental assumption of the self-medication theory: that abusers are seeking a specific effect and not just to alter their state of consciousness in a random manner. Milkman and Frosch (1973) describe the effects of heroin as "satiation" and the effect of amphetamine as "activation." Operating out of an ego psychological theoretical orientation, the investigators found significant differences between the heroin and amphetamine abusers' patterns of coping with anxiety. The heroin addict reduces anxiety by repression and withdrawal, whereas the amphetamine addict utilizes a compensatory grandiosity to maintain a posture of active engagement with the external world. Thus, the drug of choice appears to be "syntonic with the abuser's characteristic modes of adaptation" and facilitative of regressive solutions to conflict which originated in childhood. Thus, while many differences between heroin and amphetamine addicts are discussed, the basic similarity is described in the authors' conclusion to their study: "An underlying sense of low self-esteem is defended against by the introduction of a chemically-induced altered state of consciousness. The drug state helps to ward off feelings of helplessness in the face of a threatening environment. Pharmacological effect reinforces characteristic defenses which are massively deployed to reduce anxiety. Drugged consciousness appears to be a regressive state which is reminiscent of, and may recapture, specific phases of early child development" (p. 248). This hypothesis could reasonably be extended to the use of other drugs which produce similar effects, including a variety of prescription drugs. It should be noted that the authors acknowledge the importance of social factors and physiological dependence in drug abuse in addition to the defensive functions which are the focus of their study. They also recognize the possibility that the personality patterns observed in their subjects may be the result of drug use and drug lifestyle instead of factors in the development of patterns of drug use.

FREQUENCY AND COMORBIDITY OF PSYCHOACTIVE SUBSTANCE USE DISORDERS, MOOD DISORDERS, AND ANXIETY DISORDERS

In considering data on comorbidity, it must be stressed that correlational data does not determine causal relationships. A correlation is simply the probability that when one variable is present, a second variable will also be present. The variables in question here are presence of substance abuse disorders and presence of mood or anxiety disorders. The fact that the presence of one makes the presence of the other significantly more likely (a positive correlation) does not imply that substance abuse causes mood or anxiety disorders or that mood or anxiety disorders cause substance abuse disorders, although either or both may be true. It is also possible that a significant correlation may result from the effect of a third variable. Some research suggests that the gene which results in vulnerability to alcoholism is the same gene which produces vulnerability to depression. Such a gene would be the "third variable" which is "causal" of both alcoholism and depression. However, there is conflicting opinion and evidence for a separate inheritance of alcoholism. Additional well-designed research is needed to explore the causal relationships of these pervasive disorders. At present, the cause and effect relationships between psychoactive substance use disorders and psychopathology are not yet established (Frances & Allen, 1991).

Penick (cited in Frances & Allen, 1991), in a large study of male alcoholics, found that 68.5 percent of family-history positive alcoholics met the diagnostic criteria for another psychiatric syndrome besides alcoholism, whereas 51.8 percent of the family-history negative alcoholics did. Among the former group, the specific incidence of psychopathology was: depressive, 48.3%; manic, 24%; antisocial, 23.2%; panic attacks, 13.8%; drug abuse, 14.8%; obsessive compulsive, 14.3%; phobic, 11.1%; and schizophrenic, 4.6%. Keeler, Taylor, and Miller (cited in Frances & Allen, 1991) found rates of depression among recently detoxified alcoholics ranging from 8.6 to 66 percent, depending on the instrument used to measure the depression. Rounsaville, Rosenberger, Wilber, et al. (cited in Frances & Allen, 1991), in a study of narcotic addicts, found that between 9 and 42 percent met criteria for major depression, depending on the instrument used. Shuckit (cited in Frances & Allen, 1991) found that 60 percent of depressed young males had a prior substance abuse problem. He also found that among those seeking inpatient treatment, a majority had depressive symptoms secondary to alcoholism, but only 5 percent of the males and 10–15 percent of the female alcoholics had primary mood disorders. Rounsaville, Rosenberger, Wilber et al. (cited in Frances & Allen, 1991), in a study of inpatient addicts, found comorbid generalized anxiety disorder in 11 percent, phobic disorder in 5 percent, panic disorder in 3 percent, and obsessive compulsive disorder in 4 percent. Weissman, Myers, and Harding (cited in Frances & Allen, 1991), in a study of alcoholics, found generalized anxiety disorder in 9 percent and phobias in 3 percent. Crowe, Pauls, Slymen et al. (cited in Frances & Allen, 1991) found that in a sample of individuals with panic disorder, 15 percent had an alcohol disorder as compared to only 4 percent in a control group.

A great deal of valuable information about the prevalence of comorbid alcohol, other drug, and mental disorders in the United States was provided by the Epidemiologic Catchment Area (ECA) Study of Regier, et al. (1990). They analyzed data from interviews of 20,291 people in the general population, in treatment settings, and in prisons, and obtained frequency and comorbidity figures for specific psychoactive substance use disorders and other mental disorders.

The lifetime prevalence rate in the general population for a nonsubstance abuse mental disorder was 22.5 percent. For an alcohol abuse or dependence disorder, the figure was 13.5 percent of the sample. For a drug abuse or dependence disorder other than alcohol, the lifetime prevalence rate was 6.1 percent.

The comorbidity of combinations of disorders was expressed in two ways in the ECA report: as the percentage of the sample with the first disorder that also had the second disorder, and, by comparing that percentage against the percentage of the sample that had the second problem but not the first. By way of illustration, of the members of the sample that had a mental disorder, 22.3 percent had an alcohol disorder. In contrast, of the members of the sample that did not have a mental disorder, only 11 percent had an alcohol disorder. By comparing the percentages (or odds) of having an alcohol disorder, the authors derived an "odds ratio" of approximately two. Therefore, a member of the sample (and presumably the population from which the sample came) would be twice as likely to have an alcohol problem if there was a mental disorder than if there was not. Similarly, 14.7 percent of the people who had mental disorders also had another drug disorder versus 3.7 percent of the people who did not have a mental disorder. Thus, the odds ratio is about four; one is almost four times more likely to have a drug disorder if one has a mental disorder than if one does not. The comorbidity percentages and odds ratios are given in Table 7-9.

Some striking facts emerging from this table are that for individuals with a history of an alcohol disorder, the rate of mental disorders was almost double that for those without alcohol disorders. For those with alcohol disorders, the rate of other drug disorders was almost six times as great as for those without alcohol disorders. For people with a history of drug (other than alcohol) disorders, the risk of a mental disorder was four times as great; the risk of an alcohol disorder was seven times as great (among those abusing drugs, almost half also abuse alcohol).

The ECA study also provides data on the comorbidity of alcohol and other drug disorders with specific mental disorders, allowing examination of these relationships for anxiety and mood (affective) disorders. Anxiety disorders, as a group have a lifetime prevalence of 14.6 percent. There were substance abuse disorders in about one fourth, an odds ratio of 1.7. The odds ratio is considerably higher for the subgroups of panic disorder (2.9) and obsessive compulsive disorder (2.5). For all of the anxiety disorders, the odds ratios are notably higher for other drugs than for alcohol, and the psychoactive substance use disorder is much more likely to be dependence than abuse. This might be a reflection of a large amount of prescription drug dependence as a self-medicating response to anxiety.

Table 7-9. Lifetime Prevalence and Odds Ratios* of
Alcohol, Other Drug, and Mental (ADM) Disorders Among Persons
by Major ADM Disorder Groups: Five-Site ECA Combined Community
and Institutional Sample Standardized to the US Population (*After Regier, 1990*).

Comorbid Disorders	Major Disorder Groups		
	{ Any Mental Disorder, %	} No Mental Disorder, %	Odds Ratio
Any other drug	14.7**	3.7	4.5
Any alcohol	22.3**	11.0	2.3
Either alcohol or other drug	28.9**	13.2	2.7
Any mental	36.6	19.9	2.3
Any other drug	21.5**	3.7	7.1
Either mental or or other drug	45.0**	21.9	2.9
Any mental	53.1	20.1	4.5
Any alcohol	47.3**	11.3	7.1
Either mental or	71.6**	28.0	6.5

*Ratio of the odds of having the comorbid disorder (rows) in the exposed group (columns) to the odds in the nonexposed group. ECA indicates Epidemiological Catchment Area.
**P < .001

Substance abuse or dependence is found in 32.0 percent of people with a mood disorder, an odds ratio of 2.6 compared to people without a mood disorder. While rates of alcohol and other drug diagnoses are nearly equal, the odds ratios for other drug disorders are more than double those for alcohol. Rates of substance use for those with bipolar disorder are much higher than those for unipolar depression. Those with bipolar disorder are 5.6 times as likely to have an alcohol disorder and 11 times more likely to have another drug disorder than those without bipolar disorder. In addition, the rates of dependence versus abuse diagnoses are more than double the prevalence in unipolar depression, which in turn is higher than the general population. The authors comment that "These patterns raise intriguing questions regarding the relationship (i.e., causal or secondary) of substance abuse and dependence to subtypes of major affective illness" (Regier et al., 1990).

The ECA Study also provided data on comorbidity of mental disorders with specific substance abuse disorders. One or more mental disorders was found in 53.1 percent of people with a drug diagnosis (other than alcohol), 4.5 times the percentage found in people without a drug diagnosis. The most common mental disorder found in people with drug diagnoses was anxiety disorder (28.3%), with an odds ratio of 2.5. Mood disorders are 4.7 times as likely to be present in the drug abuse diagnosis group (26.4%) than in the general population.

For those individuals with alcohol disorders, 19.4 percent had anxiety disorders, an odds ratio of 1.5. 13.4 percent of individuals with alcohol disorders also had affective disorders versus 7.5 percent of those without alcohol disorders, an odds ratio of 1.9. Most strikingly, those with an alcohol disorder are five times as likely to have a bipolar disorder than those without.

It is especially important for clinical staff of treatment programs and forensic settings to be aware that, for persons who actually utilized services or were incarcerated, comorbidity is much higher even than the preceding data indicates. For persons with mental disorders seen in mental health treatment centers, the six month prevalence rate of having a substance use disorder is twice the rate of those not seeking treatment. For those treated for alcohol disorders, 55 percent have comorbid mental disorder, more than twice the rate in those with untreated alcohol disorders.

Programs and practitioners treating individuals with drug (other than alcohol) disorders are likely to find that the majority have an associated mental disorder. The ECA study found a comorbidity rate of 64.4 percent in this situation, with the odds of having a mental disorder more than four times as great for those with drug disorders who are in treatment programs (Regier et al., 1990).

CLINICAL EXAMPLES:
CASE ONE—PRIMARY DEPRESSION

Roxanne M. is a 30-year-old, black, single female who works as a respiratory therapist. She was referred by her outpatient substance abuse treatment program for psychotherapy for depression accompanied by suicidal ideation.

Both parents were born in Jamaica, were Protestant, and upper middle class. Her mother had a bipolar disorder and was treated with lithium. Her father was an alcoholic who displayed little emotional involvement with his daughter and was involved in many extramarital affairs on his frequent business travels. The parents' marriage was troubled, and after a period of intense conflict, ended in divorce when Roxanne was 12 years old. This was extremely upsetting for her and she showed signs of depression which were masked by acting out through promiscuity and drug use: speed, pep pills, cocaine, and drinking (she didn't like marijuana).

Despite her above-average ability, she was nearly expelled from her strict private school and had to repeat tenth grade. There was some attempt to address the problems through counseling, but it was evidently ineffective, as the pattern of spotty academic performance, drug abuse, promiscuity, codependent relationships, and low self-esteem continued into adulthood.

As a hospital employee, Roxanne occasionally had access to prescription drugs and developed a pattern of stealing Percocet (oxycodone and acetominophen—an opiate analgesic) because it "turned off the feelings" better than alcohol. When she was caught, her license was suspended with the possibility of reinstatement after a two-year period of successful treatment and recovery.

She entered an intensive outpatient drug and alcohol treatment program which included random, witnessed urine drug screening (UDS), and required AA/NA attendance. She did well in the program, being highly motivated by the desire to regain her ability to practice her profession, but she had difficulty bonding with the 12-step programs. When the codependent and self-destructive character of her current relationship was confronted and the pharmacological self-medication was no longer available, her depression came crashing through, accompanied by suicidal ideation. She was then referred for psychotherapy in addition to her ongoing structured program.

Psychotherapy was initially begun on a twice a week basis, and a psychiatric evaluation was done immediately. Medication was offered, but Roxanne was now resistant to a pharmacological approach to improving her mood, so it was agreed to see if response to psychotherapy alone would obviate the need. Close consultation was maintained with the primary counselor in the treatment program to insure that any negative signs would be responded to immediately. Psychotherapy was initially focused on establishing rapport and a working alliance through empathy and support accompanied by a nonjudgmental reflection of the self-destructive nature of her current relationship, which she was having difficulty ending, despite strong pressure from her treatment program to do so. An additional early aspect of the psychotherapy was the emphasis on behavioral manifestation of self-care through the systematic use of self-provided "pleasurable events." Response to psychotherapy was surprisingly rapid and dramatic. Within two weeks, Roxanne reported that feelings of depression were largely gone. She was able to quickly develop a new and positive emotional relationship with the recovery fellowships, and within four to six weeks she ended her negative relationship. While occasional brief periods of sad mood occurred, usually following interactions with her mother, she basically maintained a positive attitude and was able to begin to examine the underlying issues of her relationships with her parents.

In examining this case, a key issue is that the emotional damage leading to depression preceded the onset of substance use which was used to medicate the painful feelings. Unable to develop a stable and sustaining empathic bond with the parents due to the mother's bipolar disorder and the father's alcoholism and emotional distance, Roxanne's sense of self was seriously weakened. Drug abuse and codependent relationships were the unconscious attempt to sustain the fragile identity. Her ability to experience the psychotherapist as empathically connected to her allowed her to improve her management of anxiety and her level of self-esteem. This, in turn, allowed her to dispense with her self-destructive relationship and begin the healthy bonding with AA/NA.

CASE TWO—PRIMARY ADDICTION

Dennis O. is a 32-year-old married white male. He was referred for individual psychotherapy following a 28-day inpatient detoxification and rehabilitation treatment. Dennis' parents were both American-born Catholics of Irish ancestry. The mother was a full-time homemaker and the father was a maintenance worker who was alcoholic and emotionally abusive. During high school, Dennis began using alcohol and marijuana and, in connection with his involvement with the wrestling team, began to use diet pills (amphetamine) to help make weight limits. Following graduation, he began college on a wrestling scholarship, but left after about a year. He met his wife through a relative and married in his early twenties. The wife has a full-time job and there are no children.

After a few brief jobs, Dennis began to drive trucks, first short-haul and then long distance. Already acquainted with the effects of amphetamine, he began to use to stay awake, make deliveries on time, and to enjoy the rush and energy of a stimulant high. When he wanted to sleep, he would use alcohol. Spending long periods away from the emotional support of his wife, he began to use more drugs, adding cocaine to the mix, and drank more to come down. About five years ago, he had the first of three accidents which were to eventually cost him his job. In the first, he was hit from behind. In the second, a truck hit his from the side, with responsibility unclear. In the third, he fell asleep at the wheel, swerved off the road and crashed into the side of a cliff, narrowly escaping death. The final accident left him unemployed, plagued by chronic low back pain, and increasingly depressed. He dealt with the back pain at first with over-the-counter analgesics, and then by "doctor shopping" for pain killers, preferably Percocet. These were used more and more instead of alcohol to get to sleep as well as for pain.

A variety of short-lived unsuccessful jobs followed, with resulting financial pressures and marital strains. "Crashes" following cocaine binges and reduced sex drive stemming from the drug deepened feelings of inadequacy and depression, and one physician started him on the antidepressant Prozac (fluoxetine). He decided to try to get back into trucking and succeeded in getting a job, but the night before he was to begin a cross-country haul, he got drunk, and decided to use amphetamines to function the next day. While he managed to conceal this episode of use from his supervisor, he realized he had to stop or he would be back into the same pattern he was in before. Additionally, he knew that since 1989, random urine drug screens in the trucking industry made it impossible to get away with ongoing abuse. He spoke to a friend who was in recovery, and entered a 28-day Detox/Rehab. Treatment was very successful, and he left feeling enthusiastic and clear-headed for the first time in years. Antidepressant medication had been discontinued and was clearly no longer indicated. Follow-up psychotherapy was supportive and reality-focused, concentrating on relapse prevention, helping him utilize AA meetings and his sponsor for maximum effectiveness, and building on his new sense of self-esteem. A series of couple sessions in addition to individual sessions assisted both Dennis and his wife in modifying the formerly enmeshed and codependent relationship, and supported the wife's involvement with Alanon.

In considering the history of this case, the most salient point is the primary role of the addictions. Depression developed both from the physiological effects of the drugs and from the negative life circumstances that resulted from the addiction. Free of drugs, Dennis is euthymic most of the time. His AA attendance is regular and his sponsor is a good role model. He continues working in trucking, but only short hauls, and he has found a mentor in his company who appears to be a good-father figure. With more that a year of sobriety under his belt, he can look at the role of his dysfunctional family of origin, his emotionally abusive, self-esteem destroying father, and the former pattern of compulsive re-enactment with his wife, wherein she was placed in the role of the demeaning parent finding him inadequate. At one point in the treatment, about six months after rehab, there was a period of sad mood that prompted a referral to a psychiatrist/addictionologist; medication was not found to be necessary.

IMPLICATIONS AND CONCLUSIONS

Both substance abuse, including the subcategory of prescription drug abuse and dependence, and other psychological disorders, including mood and anxiety disorders, are pervasive and costly in our society. However, the combination of the two are far more debilitating to the individual, the family, and the larger community.

The interactions of the two categories of disorders are complex and not fully understood. Substance abuse can "mask, mimic, or result from a wide range of psychiatric and medical disorders" (Frances and Allen, 1991). Substance abuse can exacerbate an existing psychiatric disorder like bipolar disorder, manic phase, or be exacerbated by a developing psychiatric disorder.

The questions of cause and effect are an important unresolved issue, with much research support for both theories of causal directionality. Older theorists as well as many current researchers hold that there is an underlying and prior psychic distress or imbalance, perhaps biochemically-based, which renders an individual vulnerable to substance abuse and dependence because the mood-altering chemical temporarily relieved the distress, hence being more reinforcing than for those individuals who start from a position of general euthymia and serenity. The individual with primary psychological distress, as in the case of mood and anxiety disorders, would also be more likely to use and abuse prescription drugs. It would be the mood or anxiety disordered individual who would be more likely to seek medical/pharmacological assistance and would begin prescription drug use in a legitimate manner. A percentage of this population would develop abusive and possibly dependent disorders based on escalating, self-directed use. Another subgroup of prescription drug-abusing and dependent people would develop from those who have mood and anxiety disorders and discover that illegally obtained prescription drugs such as benzodiazepines can alleviate some distress. For example, an anxious individual might be offered Valium by a friend, and develop a self-medicating habit through illegal sources from the start. A third category of individual who might develop PDAD is the mood- or anxiety-disordered individual who is in a social environment in which drinking and other drug use is condoned or valued and, through experimentation, discovers that certain prescription drugs make him feel the best.

Other theorists and researchers feel that the frequently observed comorbidity of substance abuse and mood and anxiety disorders is a result of the effects of the drug abuse on mood or anxiety. In other words, substance abuse is primary, mood and anxiety disorders are secondary, and when the substance abuse is ended, the psychiatric disorder resolves quickly.

While there may be continuing debate as to the percentage of cases in which substance abuse is primary and the percentage of cases in which mood or anxiety disorders are primary, the reality is that there are many examples of both cases. The fact is that substance abuse can cause or be caused by mood or anxiety disorders, exacerbate or be exacerbated by mood or anxiety disorders, mask or be masked by mood or anxiety disorders.

There is also inconclusive evidence that both substance abuse, particularly alcoholism, and mood disorders, particularly bipolar disorder, are the common result of a common genetic predisposition. Others believe that alcoholism has a separate inheritance. In either case, the fact that both can have exacerbating effects upon the other is unquestioned. Substance abuse prevention programs should clearly include early recognition of mood and anxiety disorders among their primary efforts to avoid the development of secondary addictions. Conversely, mental illness prevention programs should include efforts aimed at early recognition of substance abuse to avoid the development of secondary mood and anxiety disorders.

Both substance abuse and depression are underrecognized and undertreated. Many individuals suffering from one or both disorders do not seek professional treatment, and sometimes, when they do, the depression or the substance abuse is missed. If both are present, sometimes only one is recognized. Since general physicians are more likely to be consulted initially than psychiatrists, the pharmacological treatment is often inadequate and ineffective; for example, antidepressants may be given at subtherapeutic levels. In addition, the need for specialized intensive treatment for substance abuse is also often missed due to patient denial or dissembling, inadequate history gathering by the physician, or unfamiliarity with the treatment continuum by the physician.

When patients with the dual diagnoses of substance abuse and mood or anxiety disorders do arrive at a treatment program designed for only substance abuse or psychiatric disorders, the treatment staff is frequently unequipped to deal with the complications of the other disorder. In particular, free standing drug and alcohol treatment programs frequently lack adequate psychiatric or psychological staff or consultants. Counselors can become frustrated by the unfamiliar complexities of the dual problems and biased against psychopharmacological treatment out of a misapplication of the abstinence principle. Similarly, in mental health treatment programs, the staff may be unfamiliar with the complicating issues of substance abuse in mood and anxiety disordered patients and programs may lack specific approaches to deal with them. The patients are frequently discharged (or never even admitted) to treatment. Treatment programs designed to deal effectively with the dual problems are few and far between, and the patients discharged from substance abuse or mental health programs because they have both problems more often end up with no treatment rather than dual diagnosis treatment. What is needed is treatment that is based on a deep understanding of both disorders, and expertise in assessing and treating both with an individualized treatment plan utilizing the variety of modalities that can contribute to positive outcomes. Woody, McLellan, Luborsky et al. (cited in Frances & Allen, 1991) found that treating psychiatric disorders along with substance abuse disorders improves outcomes for poor prognosis patients.

In summary, the causes of psychoactive substance use disorders including PDAD are multiple and complex. This is certainly also true of the causes of anxiety and mood disorders. The central issue of the causal direction of comorbid substance abuse and anxiety and mood disorders is still unresolved. It may be reasonable, given the lack of a definitive answer to this question, to assume that there are (at least) two subgroups of dual diagnosis patients: those whose mental disorder was primary and substance abuse developed in an attempt to self-medicate the symptoms, and those whose anxiety and mood disorders were a result of prolonged substance abuse which upset their neurotransmitter balance and/or their lives. In either subgroup, careful consideration must be given to the assessment and treatment of both disorders. The addictions specialist must be alert to psychiatric disorders which require special treatment in addition to addiction recovery approaches. The general psychotherapist must be sensitized to the possible coexistence of substance abuse/ dependence with presenting anxiety or mood disorders. The primary care physician must learn to recognize both types of disorders more effectively so that appropriate treatment can be delivered. Finally, while much knowledge currently available about the assessment and treatment of these disorders which can be usefully disseminated, much remains to be learned. Carefully designed and controlled empirical research is needed to explore the relative effectiveness of differing treatment approaches and combinations of treatments with different subgroups of patients.

REFERENCES

Frances, R. J. & Allen, M. H. (1991). The interaction of substance-use disorders with nonpsychotic psychiatric disorders. In R. Michels, A. M. Cooper, S. B. Guze, L. L. Judd, G. L. Klerman, A. J. Solnit, A. J. Stunkard, & P. J. Wilner (Eds.), *Psychiatry:* Vol. *1* (pp. 1–13). Philadelphia: J. B. Lippincott.

Greenfield, D. P. (1994). Prescription drug abuse and dependence: An introduction. In Greenfield, D. P. (Ed.), *Prescription Drug Abuse and Dependence,* Springfield: Charles C Thomas Publisher.

Kamerow, D. B., Pincus, H. A., & Macdonald, D. I. (1986). Alcohol abuse, other drug abuse, and mental disorders in medical practice: Prevalence, costs, recognition, and treatment. *Journal of the American Medical Association: 255:*(15), 2054–2057.

Leigh, G. (1985). Psychosocial factors in the etiology of substance abuse. In Bratter, T. E. and Forrest, G. G. (Eds.), *Substance Abuse* New York: The Free Press, pages 49–73.

Matuschka, P. R. (1985). The psychopharmacology of addiction. In Bratter, T. E. and Forrest, G. G. (Eds.), *Alcoholism and Substance Abuse* New York: The Free Press pages 49–73.

McLellan, A. T. & Druly, K. A. (1977). Non-random relation between drugs of abuse and psychiatric diagnosis. *J. Psychiat. Res., 13:* 179–184.

McLellan, A. T., Woody G. E., and O'Brien, C. P. (1979). Development of psychiatric illness in drug abusers: Possible role of drug preference. *New Engl. J. Med., 301:* 1310–1314.

Mellinger, G. D., Balter, M. B., Manheimer, D. I., Cisin, I. H., and Parry, H. J.

(1978), Psychic distress, life crisis, and use of psychotherapeutic medications: National household survey data. *Arch. Gen. Psychiat., 35:* 1045–1052.

Metzger, L. (1988). *From Denial to Recovery: Counseling Problem Drinkers, Alcoholics, and their Families.* San Francisco: Jossey-Bass.

Milkman, H. & Frosch, W. A. (1973). On the preferential abuse of heroin and amphetamine. *J. Nerv. and Mental Dis., 156:* 242–248.

Multiple Authors (1987) *Diagnostic and Statistical Manual of Mental Disorders, Third Edition, Revised,* Washington, D.C.: American Psychiatric Association. (Cite as "A.P.A., 1987").

Multiple authors (1994). *Diagnostic and Statistical Manual of Mental Disorders, Fourth Edition,* Washington, D.C.: American Psychiatric Association. (Cite as "A.P.A., 1994").

Pope, H. G. (1979). Drug abuse and psychopathology. *New Engl. J. Med., 301:* 1341–1342.

Regier, D. A., Farmer, M. E., Rae, D. S., Locke, B. Z., Dieth, S. J., Judd, L. L., and Goodwin, F. K. (1990), Comorbidity of mental disorders with alcohol and other drug abuse: Results from the epidemiologic catchment area (ECA) study. *J. Amer. Med. Assoc., 264:* 2511–2518.

Weiss, K. J. & Greenfield, D. P. (1986). Prescription drug abuse. *Psychiat. Clin. No. Amer., 9:* 475–489.

Chapter 8

AN OVERVIEW OF TREATMENT

Pamela E. Hall and Daniel P. Greenfield

INTRODUCTION

THREE TERMS:
"MODALITY," "APPROACH," AND "SETTING"

In this chapter, we will review traditional and nontraditional types of treatment available to prescription drug abusers and to other individuals with drug and alcohol problems. By way of introduction, however, and in order to avoid confusion on the part of the reader in connection with several overlapping terms, we will first define three terms. Specifically, these terms are treatment *modalities*, treatment *settings*, and treatment *approaches*. By treatment *modalities*, we refer to a concept involving a loose combination of treatment *settings* and treatment *approaches*. In our experience in reviewing the literature, the term "modality" can refer to treatment style (or approach), treatment *type* (e.g., individual, group, couples, family, and so forth), or treatment *orientation* or "school" (e.g., psychodynamic, psychoanalytic, behavioral, and so forth). Therefore, since we do not feel that this particular term has specific and intuitive meaning, we will not use it in this chapter. Instead will defer to the more specific and meaningful terms involving treatment, namely treatment *approach* and treatment *setting*.

With regard to treatment *approach*, we refer to the theoretical underpinning which the treatment professional brings to the therapeutic situation. Specific approaches include psychoanalytic, psychodynamic, supportive, counselling (advisory, in addition to psychodynamic), "client-centered," and others. A large number of such approaches or "schools" of therapy have been developed and described over the years: One encyclopedic publication identified over two-hundred-and-fifty such schools![1] For the purposes of this chapter, we use this term to identify the theoreti-

119

cal basis and—again—approach which the treating professional brings to the therapeutic situation with his/her patient or client.

Finally, we will use the term treatment *setting* in this chapter as the straightforward description of the location in which treatment takes place. Specifically, such treatment settings as inpatient, outpatient, intensive outpatient (IOP), partial hospital, day hospital, residential treatment center, rehabilitation center, and so forth are all examples of our use of this term. The settings, as will be described below, are all potentially available to prescription drug abusers and to other abusers, and in this chapter, we will describe treatment approaches and settings for such individuals.

THE PRESCRIPTION DRUG ABUSER AND OTHER DRUG AND ALCOHOL ABUSERS

A second important point to make in the context of this chapter is one that has been made before in this monograph. That is, the prescription drug abuser does not differ, in our experience, significantly from other drug abusers *except* in the way in which that individual obtains his/her drugs. Such principles of treatment as abstinence, concomitant treatment of psychiatric problems, if any, use of a combination of psychiatric and self-help approaches for treatment, and the entire range of treatment of prescription drug abusers *and* other drug abusers, apply to both types of drug abusers. The *continuum of care* which should be made available to both types of drug abusers, ranging from the most restrictive for treatment of an individual who has "hit bottom," to less intense and less restrictive treatment settings (e.g., outpatient psychotherapy with attendance at AA/NA meetings) is equally valid for both types of drug abusers. The only exception to this is the rather unique treatment setting involving rehabilitation of "impaired professionals" (e.g., impaired physicians, alcoholic attorneys, and so forth, whose drug and/or alcohol problems have reached the point of interfering with their professional work): In recent years, an "impaired professional," recovery-oriented movement has arisen in this country, identifying such individuals as impaired physicians, pharmacists, nurses, attorneys, dentists, and others (Canavan, 1983). This movement has also developed unique rehabilitation (inpatient) programs and residences for such individuals, and in the case of the health-care professional who supports his/her drug problems through prescription drug abuse, these unique settings present an exception to the continuum-of-care rule, in that such settings are specifically designated for such impaired professionals. We will discuss this further below.

SETTING THE STAGE: A CASE EXAMPLE

To set the stage for this chapter, we will present a case below which is a synthesis of a number of individuals whom the authors have treated over the years. This case will embody the principles of treatment settings and approaches which this chapter will review, and in further sections of this chapter, we will refer to this case.

Case Report

A.B., a thirty eight-year-old, separated white male, was employed as a national sales representative for a large manufacturing company. He had an extensive history of marijuana, alcohol, and cocaine use while in college, which apparently had not resulted in occupational or psychiatric problems until his present difficulties began. While traveling in connection with his work approximately four years prior to his coming to the attention of health care providers, A.B. was involved in a serious automobile accident, which resulted in severe and chronic lower lumbar back pain, without evidence of his having sustained a fracture in the accident. During the four years following that accident, A.B. had had consultations in emergency room visits for evaluation and treatment of his low back pain and resulting insomnia, irritability, depression, and headaches. For a brief period of time, this concern affected his relationship with his wife and his ten-year-old daughter (who was under his wife's custody), in that his concern seemed to bring the family closer together. However, the spiralling effects of work stress, chronic back pain, and financial problems also accelerated A.B.'s alcohol use, which he described as taking "to ease the pain and to fall asleep."

A.B. became more involved in his treatment, he acknowledged more history of drug and alcohol abuse before his accident than he had originally acknowledged. Specifically, he described a history of recreational use of alcohol, cocaine, and marijuana while in college, and described "three-martini lunches" in connection with his work. He generally did well as a sales-person, but as he gained increased responsibility and a larger number of accounts, he experienced increased anxiety and work stress when he became about thirty years old. This had ramifications on his relationship with his wife, and to help deal with these problems, he had gone to his family physician for help, particularly with his anxiety. That physician spoke with him briefly on infrequent occasions, and prescribed a high-potency benzodiazepine, which reduced his stress to some extent. However, his situation continued, essentially unchanged, up to the point of his motor vehicle accident on April 21, 1988. Following that accident, as described above, A.B. had a good deal of medical attention and treatment, almost exclusively oriented toward evaluation and treatment of his back pain, headaches, and other chronic pain syndromes, and without attention to possible emerging and worsening drug and alcohol problems.

A.B.'s situation reached the point that he was drinking heav-ily (one-to-two pints of vodka per day), and consuming excessive amounts of the prescribed benzodiazepine each week. Initially, he was able to persuade his family physician that he needed to increase the dose "just for a little while," because of work stress, difficulties with his family, and so forth. However, after several months of this duplicity, his family physician refused to renew or increase A.B.'s medication unless he came to see the doctor for regular counselling visits *and* accepted a referral to a local psychiatrist/addictionologist for treatment. A.B. declined both demands, and referred himself to a different local family physician, whose name he had obtained from a colleague at work; this second physician had the reputation in the sales community in that area as being "an easy touch for drugs..." A.B. did see this second physician, did obtain a prescription for a different benzodiazepine, as well as a renewal of the first benzodiazepine. For the next several months, A.B.'s combination of heavy drinking and excessive use of prescribed anxiolytic medications was sufficient to serve his perceived needs, until the night of his near-fatal "accident."

Early in the morning on Sunday, December 8, 1991, A.B.'s wife attempted to telephone him to arrange a schedule of visitation for that day with their son. A.B. did not answer his telephone. His wife then drove to his apartment, rang the doorbell, which was not answered. She used her key to enter the building and A.B.'s apartment, and when she entered his bedroom, she found him comatose in bed, with three almost completely empty bottles of pills at his bedside, along with a quart bottle of vodka which was about one-third full. There was no suicide note or other indication of suicide or foul play, and A.B.'s wife immediately telephoned the local rescue squad, which took him to the local hospital's emergency room for evaluation and treatment. A.B. was determined to be in coma, and he was hospitalized acutely on the intensive care unit (ICU) of the hospital, where he underwent dialysis and was maintained on life support systems. He regained consciousness after about two days, and described that he had a black-out for the period of time leading up to his apparent overdose; whether or not this overdose was intentional or unintentional, was a suicide gesture or simply an effort on his part to "get rid of that awful headache," was a question which was never answered. Shortly after regaining consciousness, A.B. experienced a combined alcohol-sedative withdrawal syndrome (similar to the D.T.'s), which was treated effectively with a long-acting oral benzodiazepine, and after an uneventful hospitalization from the medical perspective, he was to have been discharged after five days of hospitalization.

Psychiatric consultation for A.B. was obtained on his fourth day of hospitalization. The consultant, along with the staff Certified Alcohol Counsellor (CAC)—who was also involved in psychiatric consultation for drug and alcohol questions—advised A.B. that they felt he had a serious unresolved alcohol and prescription drug abuse problem; that in their opinion, his overdose may well have been intentional (even though he claimed he could not remember having felt that way at the time); and that inpatient treatment was necessary for him and was their recommendation. A.B. acknowledged that he had once had such a problem, but that he had "learned (my) lesson from this overdose," and that he felt that he had "my problem under control . . . " He disagreed with the consultants' recommendation, and insisted on leaving the hospital as soon as possible, against medical advice (AMA), if necessary. The possibility of involuntary hospitalization for probable suicidal intent was discussed, and A.B. finally accepted a referral to a local drug and alcohol rehabilitation program. A.B. was particularly willing to accept that referral after a "structured intervention" (a confrontation concerning the need for treatment for his active drug and alcohol problem, attended by his treating physician in the hospital, his treating physician outside, his wife and son, his supervisor at work, a close friend, and the consulting psychiatrist and CAC in the hospital) was done at his bedside on the day he would otherwise have been discharged to go home.

At his rehabilitation program, a traditional recovery-oriented, twenty-eight-day, inpatient rehabilitation program with professional supervision, A.B. had a difficult first week because of his denial. However, the continuing pressure and support from the treating staff and the patient groups did encourage him to stay and to work through the program, which he did. Although he was discharged uneventfully, during the last week of the program, the treating staff did not feel that his recovery was sufficiently strong to permit him to be discharged to a relatively unstructured treatment setting. Therefore, A.B. was to continue in the intensive outpatient program (IOP) affiliated with a psychiatric hospital near his home. His participation in that program was generally good in terms of attendance and compliance, and he participated in the initial phase of treatment (several-hour treatment sessions, including group and individual therapy four evenings per week, after work), then in the less intense phase of that program (a similar format, twice per week), and then finally completing the IOP after a four-month, once-per-week program. During all of this time, A.B. was to attend AA/NA meetings on his own when he was not attending the IOP. He did, with generally good attendance and compliance at these meetings, and he did earn his "ninety-day" pin by having attended ninety AA/NA meetings in ninety days following his discharge from the hospital.

After completing the IOP over a period of about a year, with the help and support of the treating staff in that program, A.B. accepted a referral from that program for outpatient aftercare treatment with a psychiatrist/addictionologist in his community. This treatment has been productive and useful for A.B., and is continuing as of this writing. The psychiatrist's approach with A.B. has been behavioral, and recognizing A.B.'s tendency to attempt to resolve his problems through pharmacologic means, he has avoided all psychoactive medications with A.B. in his own treatment. This has been a useful follow-through for A.B., who has been drug-free (prescription drug or otherwise) since the night of his overdose, notwithstanding his urges and cravings for "pharmacologic help" (using his words). A.B.'s problems with his work, his pain syndrome, his wife and son, and his other daily problems have been continuing, although there have been some useful breakthroughs, particularly with regard to his pain syndrome. As of this writing, A.B. continues to be involved in formal treatment and recovery groups on a regular and active basis.

Inherent in the description of A.B.'s situation is a good deal of material having to do with treatment approaches and treatment settings. Using this case as a springboard for discussion of treatment approaches and settings, the rest of this chapter will present discussions of these various treatment approaches and treatment settings.

Treatment Approaches

Several approaches are currently utilized in the treatment of substance abuse. Most programs will offer a combination of various approaches depending upon the level of staff expertise, phase of treatment, and individual philosophy of the treatment setting. There is no one preferred approach to treatment, and generally all of the following approaches hold some validity in terms of assisting addicted individuals toward recovery, regardless of whether their addiction is "licit" (PDAD) or "illicit" (street drugs). It is true, however, that insights into the problem of addiction. We recommend utilizing a variety of approaches when treating the chemically-dependent individual.

Group Therapy

Group therapy is a frequently used approach basic to most addiction treatment settings today, particularly inpatient and intensive outpatient programs (IOP's). There are several advantages to this approach, including peer feedback and support, a high propensity for group confrontation, and the benefits of peer pressure to remain in recovery. Group approaches also break ground on building a new friendship network for patients who are being prevailed upon to often surrender many of their past associations.

There are several variations on group treatment. These include groups for substance abusers only; codependent groups for family members and/or significant others; multifamily groups; and groups that address a specific problem such as chronic relapse. (These are sometimes known as "slippers" groups.) The value of these groups depends largely on the ability of the group leaders to facilitate properly relevant discussions on critical topics and to mediate confrontations in therapy groups so that they remain therapeutic and do not become destructive (Yalom, 1975).

Self-help programs like AA and NA work on the premise of group intervention. They openly recognize the power of "the group" to effect certain positive changes. This power is indeed true, given the noteworthy success record of the self-help, recovery-oriented, "anonymous" programs. Groups are most effective when they are kept focused and when they adopt specific rules to assist in the self-monitoring of the participants (e.g., no cross-conversation, no acting out, and so forth) (Gurman & Razin, 1977).

Group treatment lends itself to interactive and experiential exchanges that cannot be obtained through any other approach to treatment. Many gestalt techniques such as the "empty chair" and psychodrama exercises are very effective in the group therapeutic approach. Last, it is quite clear that people gain a certain important degree of validation when they witness others' struggling with the same problems in recovery as their own.

Relapse prevention groups meet less frequently than intensive psychotherapy groups at the beginning of treatment, but these latter groups are an essential part of aftercare. Relapse prevention groups deal with specific long-term issues and stresses encountered in living an actively-recovering lifestyle. These groups provide a solid resource to the successfully recovering individual in need of ongoing guidance. There will always be new pressures and traumas which occur despite the patient's genuine efforts to get well, simply because life is a constant ebb and flow of such distresses. The practical focus of relapse prevention addresses issues of maintaining and preserving long-term sobriety.

DWI (driving while intoxicated) groups serve a critical purpose as a frequent "front-line" experience for the chemically-addicted adult. These groups typically employ an educative focus in an attempt to inform the identified patients of their addictive tendencies. It is the "first step" that begins the confrontation process which will, in turn, hopefully lead to eventual intensive addiction treatment. Many individuals, unfortunately, are unable to cease their use of chemicals, despite the multimedia appeal of the usual DWI groups which employ heart-wrenching videos, movies and stories of the fatalities involving impaired motorists. DWI interventions are still essential because the experience of the group will eventually become "factored into" the overall chemical abuse history that constitutes the core of the patient's addiction. At some point it is hoped that the individual will need to face and recognize his or her pattern of problems due to substance abuse and seek the treatment required.

Family Therapy

This approach is frequently used in addiction services, and is often especially useful in work with adolescent addicts. Family involvement is crucial in the treatment of all chemically-addicted patients, especially in the treatment of the prescription drug abuser who may be consuming his/her drug of choice with long-standing corresponding family sympathy for the symptoms of aches, pains, depression, anxiety, and so forth, which the prescribed medications are supposed to treat (Hester and Miller, 1989). Such individuals face a special problem with "enabling" from their loved ones because for many years, the substances abused by the addict were viewed by the family members as "necessary" medications for chronic pain, psychiatric syndromes, and other such disorders. These family members will need special assistance to resist the enabler role despite possible desperate pleas from their loved ones for "medication." Family therapy can also help to address many of the crisis-related problems that arise from chronic addiction such as loss of job, house, or substantial financial, or legal problems (Hester and Miller, 1989).

Multi-Family Groups allow both the family members and patients to see their pattern of maladaptive behaviors repeated in other families outside their own. This is a powerful approach because "one picture is worth a thousand words." When families can see their patterns in others, that awareness sends a clear message about the nature of pathology, and the ways in which family members affect each other by their behaviors, attitudes, verbalizations, and so forth.

Marital Therapy

Marital or couples therapy is used episodically throughout various treatment settings. Ten to fifteen sessions is the usual time-limited framework employed by many therapists (Hester and Miller, 1989). This approach is most valuable at a point when recovery is in progress because addiction often produces a great deal of damage to the trust and commitment aspects of the relationship; good recovery ameliorates this damage. These hurts need to be resolved, but they do require a certain amount of expression of anger and ventilation on the parts of both spouses. Confrontation is most effective when the recipient is committed to recovery and is willing to assume responsibility for his/her actions without retreating into substance abuse. Sexual issues may also need to be addressed, and should be done in this format rather than any group interactive effort.

There are many tasks in family and marital therapy to be accomplished. Reducing the drinking pattern of a spouse can assist in not enabling or triggering the person in recovery to relapse. Couples need to be guided toward building a synergy of more caring behaviors toward each other to replace the abusive angry interactions that once dominated their interchange. People also benefit from some practical retraining in communications skills. Several studies have documented that multiple couples group are quite successful and meet with positive patient feedback (Hester and Miller, 1989). Marital therapy or such a group can be an effective addition to individual therapy efforts concerning addiction.

Patterns of past physical, mental, and/or emotional abuse must be covered in this marital intervention approach. This is best accomplished by inquiring directly about such incidents. Abuse issues may exist in the present marital relationship, may extend back to early childhood or both. New methods for anger expressions and resolution in addition to modifications in communication styles may bring about significant improvements in the marital relationship (Potter-Efron and Potter-Efron, 1991). A potential for physical violence must always be specifically assessed. When there is a strong chance for such abuse, the therapist must take action to provide for the safety and protection of all minor children and/or abused spouses as the first priority.

Psychopharmacotherapy

Finally, as an adjunct—but not a substitute—for the other therapeutic approaches to the treatment of PDAD patients and other "illicit" drug users, psychopharmacotherapy can play an important role (AA, 1984). Paradoxically, psychoactive medications (described in detail in Chapter 2) are the agents which are sought by PDAD patients, and which "get them in trouble" in the first place. In addition, psychoactive, or psychotropic, medications can in many instances be obtained illicitly (i.e., for present purposes, "on the street," and not through diversion from physicians' practices), and therapy can be considered as both "licit" and "illicit" sources of drug abuse: The psychopharmacologic agents and their central nervous system (CNS) effects are the same, regardless of how they are obtained. As therapeutic agents, however, which are often used and sometimes essential for the treatment of PDAD and other drug abusers (especially "dual diagnosis" patients), psychopharmacologic agents can be divided into six groups, all of which have "anti-" groups and are presented in the Table 8-1.

In the case of the "dual diagnoses" patient, in which patients self-medicate to reduce the intensity of their symptomatology, patients may divert prescribed medications from their physicians, or other prescribers' practices for that purpose initially, and may then find themselves dependent on those medications. Of all six groups of "anti-" psychotropic medications, that pattern happens in our experience most frequently with antianxiety medications, especially benzodiazepines.

In the case of patients with acute and chronic pain syndromes, diversion from Schedule II (see Chapter 1) CDS drugs (especially opiates) is a frequent occurrence, and conversely, Schedule II CDS is a class of drugs for which physicians are frequently disciplined by licensing authorities (Greenfield, 1984). Since these drugs are also popular "on the street," it is sometimes difficult clinically to distinguish between "iatrogenic" (i.e., physician caused) addiction and "street" addiction among PDAD patients whose drugs of choice are the opiates. Such a distinction becomes critical in psychotherapy, especially with regards to assessing a patient's motivation to stop using drugs.

In addition to these two aspects of psychopharmacotherapy—uses of psychotropic medications to treat symptoms arising from psychiatric disorders ("dual diagnosis" patients), and use of analgesics (especially opiates) in iatrogenic and/or "street" patterns of abuse and dependence—a

Table 8-1. Six "Anti-" Groups of Psychotropic Medications.

GROUP	PSYCHIATRIC DISORDER(S)	EXAMPLES*
Anti-psychotic ("neuroleptic") agents	Psychosis; Schizophrenia; Toxic (drug-induced) organic brain syndromes	Phenothiazines (Thorazine®, Stelazine®, Prolixin®), Haldol®, Navane®, Clozaril®, others
Anti-anxiety ("anxiolytic") agents	Anxiety disorders; Panic disorders	Benzodiazepines (Valium®, Librium®, Xanax®, Serax®, Tranxene®, Halcion®), Miltown®, Equanil® barbiturates, Buspar®, others
Anti-manic ("mood-stabilizing") agents	Bipolar ("manic-depressive") disorders; Hypomania	Lithium compounds; Tegretol®, Depakote®, others
Anti-depressant ("thymoleptic") agents	Major depressive disorder: Dysthymia	Tricyclics (Elavil®, Tofranil®, Sinequan®, others); Prozac®, Desyrel®, Ludiomil®, Zoloft®, Wellbutrin® other
Anti-pain ("analgesic") agent	Acute and chronic pain syndrome	Opiate (narcotic) agents (morphine, Demerol®, Dilaudid®, Fentanyl® etc.), anti-inflammatory agents (aspirin, Butazolidin, etc.), and others
Anti-seizure ("anti-convulsant") agents	Seizure disorders	Dilantin®, Tegretol®, Mysoline®, barbiturates, others

*Brand names are given, where indicated.

third type of psychopharmacotherapeutic intervention can frequently be useful for alcoholics. That intervention involves the use of Disulfiram (Antabuse) with alcoholics (not, strictly speaking, PDAD patient/clients, although "dual addiction" with alcohol and other substances, especially benzodiazepines, is a frequent occurrence [National Institute on Drug Abuse; 1990] in the clinical care of addicts and alcoholics) who are sufficiently motivated to take some Antabuse tablet (250 mg.) per day

(Wallace, 1987). If a patient does this and then drinks alcohol, he or she will experience the "Alcohol-Antabuse reaction," characterized by an hypertension crisis, headache, nausea and vomiting, malaise, and a profound feeling of sickness. The prospect of this reaction, in turn, serves as a stimulus for the motivated alcoholic to take his/her Antabuse medication daily, and as a deterrent for him/her not to drink alcohol when "under the influence" of Antabuse.

Finally, in situations where PDAD or "illicit" drug abusers are actually under the influence of, or intoxicated with, CDS or other psychoactive substances, psychoactive medications which are "cross-reactive" (pharmacologically similar) to the intoxicating substances may have to be given the intoxicated individual to safely remove the intoxicating substance.

The principle of detoxification is to use a cross-reactive pharmacologic agent that can be carefully and systematically administered to an intoxicated individual to "substitute" for the actual drug of intoxication, then gradually and over time, to reduce the amount of the detoxifying agent to nothing, as the individual undergoes safe and gradual detoxification. This then avoids a sudden withdrawal syndrome resulting from the sudden cessation of the intoxicating drug.

Detoxification should be done under medical supervision in a structured medical setting (hospital or emergency service setting), in order to monitor vital signs and other physiologic signs and thereby assure the medical safety of the individual undergoing detoxification. Examples include the use of benzodiazepines (Librium®, Serax®, etc.) to detoxify an individual from alcohol and methadone to detoxify an individual from heroin or other opiates.

Regardless of the actual psychopharmacotherapeutic intervention used with particular PDAD or other drug abusing patients, we emphasize the point we made at the beginning of this section of this chapter—that psychopharmacotherapy with these individuals should be an adjunct (sometimes a very important, or even essential adjunct) for other therapeutic approaches to treatment, and not a substitute for them.

Individual Therapy

The individual therapy approach to addiction treatment is an essential part of the recovery process. Programs which exclude individual therapy for the sake of cost-effectiveness also compromise the potential for long-term recovery in their patients. It is generally accepted among therapists and other healthcare providers that the greatest element of effectiveness in therapy is the quality of the relationship between the therapist and the patient (Cameron, 1963). The single most helpful aspect of the self-help "anonymous" programs is also this personal alliance built between the addicted individual and his/her sponsor.

Individual therapy affords an opportunity for the patient to reveal aspects of his/her personal life and past history which may not be able to be revealed in a group format. Contrary to the beliefs of some, there are many issues which are most appropriately left for exploration in the privacy of the individual treatment relationship. A strong interpersonal connection between a patient and therapist serves to inspire continued commitment to treatment goals as designed together with the therapist's help.

Individual therapists employ a variety of theoretical constructs in the course of their therapy efforts with patients. Some therapists choose to follow a specific clearly defined theoretical framework, while others offer a more flexible, eclectic form of treatment interventions. In our experience, no single optimal approach to individual therapy exists. However, individual therapy is generally best if both the therapist and patient feel a high degree of comfort with the type of treatment approach being employed, as well as with each other.

Treatment approaches which focus on the individual are numerous. One such technique behavior therapy, includes such concepts as techniques contingency reinforcement schedules, systems of rewards and consequences, and behavioral contracting around certain issues such as refraining risky relapse behaviors. Specific focus on particular behaviors is often useful in offering rapid and usually long-lasting reduction of such dangerous or unhealthy actions. The patient's willingness to commit to the behavioral contract is essential. The eventual positive results of their commitment often empowers the person to see what he or she can achieve with a strong commitment in a positive behavioral plan.

Specific sensitization scenes can be constructed to help induce nausea or to elicit intense negative emotional responses such as disgust, fear, embarrassment and/or anxiety. Adversive images paired with the concept of substance abuse can often be effective in helping to reduce chemical addiction behavior. Patients can eventually learn to imagine escaping from a tempting situation or avoiding the situation altogether. In behavioral therapy, the patients become active participants in their own treatment process. They are encouraged to engage in self-monitoring; setting up personal systems of rewards; studying what benefits substance abuse has brought; and then substituting these perceived benefits with alternative coping strategies to meet these same needs.

There are many behavioral strategies and interventions too numerous to describe fully. All assertiveness training techniques, implosion and flooding with anxiety-provoking stimuli, and various operant conditioning punishment procedures (self-/or drug-induced nausea) comprise a wide selection of variations on behavioral interventions (Morse and Watson, 1977). Biofeedback is yet another behavioral intervention which combines the tenets of behavior therapy with physiological measures of response produced by the body. This is an extremely effective tool, assisting patients to reduce their levels of stress and anxiety, which levels are in turn a prime causal factor in chronic substance abuse and relapse. Biofeedback can be employed as a primary treatment focus or as an ancillary treatment combined with both individual and group/family therapeutic contacts. In any combination, biofeedback is a powerful additional support for patients to use in times of fears of relapse, of avoiding business pressures, etc. All behavior therapy including biofeedback is usually specific, time-limited, and practical in focus.

Psychodynamic and psychoanalytic approaches focus on issues of a patient's past experience in childhood. This is particularly useful in assessing the possibility of early childhood trauma and/or sexual abuse issues. In addition, this approach can help to identify the link between present and past behaviors. It assists in exposing issues of repressed resentment, hostility, and anxiety that often lead to relapse if left unresolved. This conceptualization can help the therapist identify a patient's defense mechanisms and levels of unconscious motivation. The overall goal is to restructure the character of the person through reliving and explaining past childhood events (Corey, 1977).

The patient-centered approach developed by Carl Rogers (1939) and the rational-emotive techniques of Albert Ellis (1962) both hold value in work with addictive patients. The patient-centered approach is less confrontive and serves to convey a sense of confidence in one's patient. This confidence is often an intensely effective intervention to help build self-esteem and motivate the patient to commit to recovery.

A patient-centered style can also rechannel a lot of the usual anger and hostility in the addicted patient into more productive means of recovery rather than setting up an authoritarian blockade of resisting what they are being advised to do. This is a common therapeutic impasse when dealing with patients in addiction that can be effectively dismantled in a patient-centered approach.

The rational-emotive technique epitomizes a confrontive style which is synonymous with addiction treatment. This stance in individual therapy will challenge the patient to new levels of awareness and will foster the skills necessary to be able to monitor and criticize his/her behavior and irrational beliefs. It attacks manipulation and excuse-making rationale directly.

As mentioned previously, there are too many theoretical approaches to treatment to discuss all of them in detail. A recent encyclopedic test, for example, described 250 such approaches (Herink, 1980). In this section of this chapter, we have outlined some of the most basic, proven, and globally adopted approaches to treatment intervention, at the same time commenting on the value of each approach. As therapists, our role is to educate and inform our patients of the options available to them and of the benefits offered to them by each treatment approach. This effort, alone, begins to draw the patient into his/her *own* treatment process rather than allowing him/her to continue to feel excluded from the treatment process.

TREATMENT SETTINGS

Several treatment settings are available to the PDAD and the "illicit" drug-abusing patient in which various therapeutic approaches to recovery can be delivered. Individual treatment efforts traditionally offer the first effort to assist the addicted patient. A confrontation or structure intervention by a family physician who has noticed a pattern of prescription drug abuse and resulting declining health might be the first such step to treatment.

As with A.B., a large number of patients will then be referred to an individual therapist, such as a psychologist, psychiatrist, social worker, certified alcohol counselor, registered nurse in clinical practice, pastoral counselor, etc. These professionals attempt to diagnose the condition of chemical dependency through clinical interviews/observation and/or family report, and so forth. One significant benefit of remaining solely in private individual treatment at that point is privacy: Many patients are initially resistant to any group treatment effort or inpatient rehabilitation program because of fear of embarrassment and humiliation, or fear of the disruption rehabilitation placement creates on an individual's daily routine and responsibilities. Most patients wish their treatment to remain strictly confidential. They may be unwilling to allow people at their place of work to become aware (through, for example, third party insurance billing) of their efforts to recover from drug and/or alcohol problems.

Often, the individual therapist is the patient's only link to recovery. In such instances, it is imperative for the therapist to continue to work toward peer support and self-help ancillary support groups for those times when the therapist is not available. This process may take a considerable amount of time and effort, but it remains a central goal for long-term treatment. As the patients become stronger in their education and awareness of addiction, they may lose some of the initial embarrassment and hopefully open themselves up to more peer support and group treatment experiences.

Along with treating nonmedical mental health professionals, psychiatrists may have several patients in their practices for purposes of medication monitoring. Among such a population are hidden prescription drug abusers which will test the clinical acumen of that physician. The unique biological and psychological expertise psychiatrists possess are their best weapon in identifying such patients, along with their being willing to take the necessary time to assess continually the patients in their own practices as well as those referred for medication monitoring.

Inpatient Programs

There is a tremendous variety of treatment programs now available throughout the United States. This variety is positive in the sense that treatment for such a frequent malady, which affects people of all races, classes, and cultures, is now commonplace and less stigmatized. A problem, on the other hand, with such a varied selection of treatment settings is that it becomes a challenge to select the most appropriate program for a given patient's specific concerns.

Twenty-eight and forty-two day rehabilitation programs provide an intensive focus on detoxification and recovery. The educational component in such programs is usually strong, so that when the patient is discharged he or she hopefully has a new clear direction about the road to recovery and about what is required of him or her on a long-term basis to maintain that recovery. These programs take people away from their everyday pressures and provide a respite for reflection, personal self-study, and recovery. A disadvantage to that respite, however, is that the patient must eventually return home to face all the same issues which pressured him or her initially. Hopefully, while "clean," such patients can begin to employ the techniques of the program they have learned.

Open-ended rehabilitation programs can provide a longer and more complete recovery experience. However, these are nearly nonexistent because of this rising costs of medical care and the pressure of healthcare providers to discharge patients as soon as progress is noted. The opposite end of the spectrum from open-ended programs is the five to seven day brief detoxification programs which manage the detoxification process throughout the day, then permit the patient to return home in the evening. This protocol can reduce hospitalization costs tremendously.

Outpatient Programs

In the same vein of cost-saving, the spectrum of outpatient recovery programs was born. This model is currently widely used program with different treatment approaches for chemical dependency of all kinds. Intensive outpatient programs (IOP's) require strict attendance at a multidisciplinary program four nights weekly; a self-help commitment on the one night off per week from treatment is also required. IOP's can produce excellent results with many individuals who are also still able to maintain their full-time jobs and their personal integrity. Such patients are confronted with handling the daily life problems from which they cannot escape, except temporarily in an inpatient setting. While this confrontive style may be difficult at first for patients, it also allows the patient to develop realistic and effective coping techniques for these frequent daily pressures.

Another outpatient stage of treatment is Aftercare. This follow-up to the IOP stage is prescribed with some concurrent individual therapy which is expected on a regular basis. This affords continued contact with a peer group, but also allows the patient to develop a strong positive therapeutic adjustment process and recovery-maintenance issues. Follow-up treatment is a critical phase because many patients perceive themselves as "cured" once they complete their initial treatment effort. It is essential there be a heavy emphasis on the importance of follow-up therapy as it is equally important in the overall recovery process.

Partial Hospital Programs

The partial hospital treatment model is another setting in which patients can receive several group encounters and build peer support.

They are removed from the pressures of their daily life because they must attend the scheduled treatment sessions, but they must also learn to deal with the ongoing life and family issues. Day-hospital programs have give way to IOP's, which is the same concept, only conducted at night. There are some individuals, however, who may need the additional protective environment and decreased pressure provided by a nontraditional day hospital setting. This will include individuals with a concurrent suicide attempt, major depression, or extensive medical problems from a complicated detoxification process.

Residential Programs

Finally, in the area of *residential* programs, we note a new trend for the treatment of impaired professionals (McBride, 1992), who may be psychologist, physicians, counselors, pharmacists, attorneys, social workers, and so forth. This new trend of residential centers for such impaired individuals recognizes the supportive nature of such congregate living arrangements as well as the cost-effective aspects of residential facilities.

CONCLUSION

In this chapter we have presented descriptions of the various services available to PDAD patients and to other addicted and alcoholic individuals. We have discussed similarities and differences between these treatment approaches and settings. Each type of treatment is valuable in its own right, however, so that in our experience, a critical factor for successful treatment should be to assist the patient in deciding and committing to a preferred treatment of choice.

REFERENCES

Alcoholics Anonymous (1984). "The A.A. Member and Medications" (pamphlet), New York: A.A. General Services.

Cameron, N. (1963). *Personality Development and Psychopathology.* Boston: Houghton-Mifflin.

Canavan, D. (1983). The Subject of Impairment. *Journal of the Medical Society of New Jersey, 80:* 47–48.

Carey, G. (1977). *Theory and Practice of Counseling and Psychotherapy.* Belmont, Ca: Wadsworth.

Ellis, A. (1962). *Reason and Emotion in Psychotherapy,* New York: Lyle Stewart.

Greenfield, D., "Controlled Dangerous Substances Prescribing Practice." Grand Rounds presented at Essex County Hospital Center, April 13, 1984.

Greenfield, D., "Psychopharmacology in the Practice of Internal Medicine." Medical Staff Conference presented at Montefiore Medical Center/Albert Einstein College of Medicine, October 22, 1988.

Gurman, A.S. and Razin, A.M. (1977). *Effective Psychotherapy: A Handbook of Research.* New York: Pergamon Press.

Herink, J. *The Psychotherapy Handbook: The A–Z Guide to More than 250 Different Therapies in Use Today* (1980), N.Y.: New American Library.

Hester, R.K. and Miller, W.R. (1989). *Handbook of Alcoholism Treatment Approaches: Effective Alternatives.* New York: Pergamon Press.

McBride, H. (1992). Personal communication.

Morse, S. and Watson, R.I., Jr. (1977). *Psychotherapies: A Comparative Casebook.* New York: Holt, Rinehart, and Winston.

National Institute of Drug Abuse, "Annual Emergency Room Data 1990," Drug Abuse Warning Network (DAWN) Statistical Series (Series I, Number 10-A), Washington: USDHHS, NDA, 1990.

Potter-Efron, R.T. and Potter-Efron, P.S. (1991). *Anger, Alcoholism and Addiction: Treating Individuals, Couples and Families.* New York: W.W. Norton.

Chapter 9

LEGAL DISPOSITIONS AND INTERVENTIONS

David A. Schwartz and Daniel P. Greenfield

Prescription drug abuse and dependence (PDAD) can lead to civil and criminal liability for the abuser and the provider/prescriber. The system of laws which address the criminal use (unlawful possession) of prescription drugs is remarkably undetailed and arcane.

In contrast, providing prescription drugs to the ultimate user by various licensed medical professionals is the subject of an often elaborate and complicated regulatory scheme which is designed to narrowly define the circumstances under which an individual can lawfully obtain prescription drugs, and to provide for license revocation and suspension for violation of the regulations. Within the epidemiologic triangle of "host, agent, and environment"—which is the paradigm for this monograph—this chapter will focus on the criminal disposition of patients who are convicted of the illegal possession of prescription drugs (the environment), and the regulatory scheme governing the various prescribers and medical practitioners who make prescription drugs available in the environment. The contrasts of both fields of legislation present markedly divergent views within the context of prevention and punishment. The regulations which control the making and administration of prescriptions cover the entire spectrum of potential conduct by practitioners. The laws relating to the disposition of individuals who are convicted of possession of prescription drugs are, in comparison, lacking in any specific consideration of the mitigating circumstances which usually accompany prescription drug abuse.

LEGAL ASPECTS AND INTERVENTIONS

Sentencing Dispositions for Prescription Drug Offenders

The Uniform Controlled Substances Act (hereinafter "UCSA") as enacted in 1970 and 1990, has been adopted in all 50 States with some variation which deal mainly with the classification and description of prohibited conduct. A provision of the UCSA which has received uniform adoption in every state is the categorization of controlled substances ("controlled dangerous substances, or "CDS") within five Schedules (I–V; Table 9-1).[1]

The classification scheme embodied in Schedules I through V appears to function as a sliding scale in which criminal punishment is most severe for violations involving the most "dangerous" substances (Schedule I) to the least severe for the least "dangerous" controlled substances (Schedule V). It is generally recognized in the law that the possession and use of prescription drugs is a less serious offense than possession of crack, cocaine, heroin or other illicit substances. Therefore, the typical sentencing rubric found in our survey of state drug sentencing laws reveals that the severity of punishment in terms of imprisonment and fines declines in a steady progression from Schedule I through V in a linear fashion. The majority of criminal sentences meted out for individuals convicted of illegal possession of prescription drugs (CPS) are for the substances found within Schedules IV and V of the UCSA. Table 9-2 presents examples of all five schedules, including Schedules IV and V.

No state makes any specific statutory provision for sentencing an individual convicted of the illegal possession of a prescription drug. For example, Mississippi provides that for a conviction for simple possession (as opposed to possession with intent to distribute) of a Schedule I or Schedule II substance (except marijuana), a person can be sentenced to no more than three years of imprisonment. In contrast, simple possession of Schedule III, IV, and V substances carries a term of imprisonment of not more than one year. Georgia law provides that possession of a controlled substance in Schedule I or a *narcotic drug* in Schedule II shall carry a sentence no fewer than 2 years and no more than 15 years imprisonment. On the other hand, simple possession of a controlled substance under Schedule III, IV, and V carries a sentence of no less than one year and no more than five years. Massachusetts directly correlates its drug sentencing provisions to classes of controlled substances for the purpose of establishing penalties (Section 31 of the Massa-

**Table 9-1. Bases for Assignment and Prescribing Requirements
for Controlled Prescription Drugs.**

Schedule	Basis for Assignment	Prescribing Requirements
I	The drug or other substance has (1) a high potential for abuse; (2) no accepted medical use in U.S.; and (3) a lack of accepted safety for medical use	Not prescribable by private physicians
II	The drug or other substance has (1) a high potential for abuse; (2) an accepted medical use; and (3) potential for severe psychological or physical dependence	Prescriptions must be signed and given adequate identifying patient information; must bear the federal DEA (and state equivalent) registration number of the prescriber; must be limited in quantity to a 30-day or 120-dose supply (whichever is less); may not be telephoned, except in very unusual circumstances
III	The drug or other substance has (1) a potential for abuse less than Schedule I or II substances; (2) an accepted medical use; and (3) potential for moderate or low physical or psychological dependence	Prescriptions must be signed and given adequate identifying patient information; must bear prescriber's DEA number; may be refilled five five times or for a 6-month period (whichever comes first); may be telephoned; no limit on quantity
IV	The drug or other substance has (1) a potential for abuse less than Schedule III substances; (2) an accepted medical use; and (3) limited potential for physical or psychological dependence	Same as for Schedule III
V	The drug or other substance has (1) a potential for abuse less than Schedule IV substances; (2) an accepted medical use; and (3) potential for dependence less than other four Schedules	Same as for Schedules III and IV except they (1) may be refilled for up to one year and (2) are available without prescription under certain circumstances

Table 9-2. Controlled Prescription Drugs, Federal Schedules.

Class of Drug	Schedule I	Schedule II	Schedule III	Schedule IV	Schedule V
Hallucinogens	Marijuana LSD	—	—	—	—
Stimulants	Congeners of amphetamines	Amphetamine Methamphetamine	Mazindol Phendimetrazine Other anorexiants	Diethylpropin Phentermine	—
Narcotic analgesics	Heroin 1-alpha acetyl methadol (LAAM)	Codeine Methadone Oxycodone Morphine	Combination such as APC + codeine, ASA + codeine		
Depressants		Amobarbital Secobarbital	Glutethimide Unscheduled drug + amobarbital and so forth	All benzodiazepines	Mixtures containing small quantities of narcotics, generally for anti-tussive and anti-diarreheal purposes. Available under some circumstances without prescription.

chusetts Controlled Substances Act is titled "Classification of Controlled Substances for the Purposes of Establishing Penalties"). Section 31 establishes five classes of penalties (A through E) which coordinate to Schedules I through V of the UCSA.

Texas, Arkansas, Rhode Island, New Jersey and Oregon also provide for a declining scale of prison terms which correlate to the various schedules of controlled substances under the UCSA.

Typically, a sentence in a criminal case will include a provision for a term of imprisonment within a range of years or months (e.g., 3–5 years or 11 ½–23 months). In the alternative, a term of imprisonment may be a sentence from 0 through 5 years, which is otherwise known as a "flat sentence". A flat sentence does not require serving a minimum mandatory term of imprisonment before a defendant is eligible for parole.

Under either circumstance (a range of years term or a flat sentence), the drug abuser who is convicted of unlawful possession of a prescribed (CDS) substance has the opportunity to reduce a potential sentence to a minimum by raising mitigating factors which caused or lead to their possession and illegal abuse of the prescription drug. New Jersey, Michigan, and Indiana, among other states, allow for the proof of mitigating and aggravating factors which will determine the time period of imprisonment within a particular range sentence or within a particular flat sentence. New Jersey sentencing provisions allow for the inclusion of mitigating factors which would rise to the level of "substantial grounds tending to excuse or justify the Defendant's conduct although failing to establish a defense to the charge." This mitigating factor has been used with some degree of success in drug offenses. Other mitigating factors are that the defendant's conduct neither caused nor threatened serious harm (in that the possession of certain controlled substances is a "victimless crime"), and that the defendant is likely to respond to probationary treatment (*see* N.J.S.A. 2C:44-1 *et. seq.*). Michigan law allows "departures" under its sentencing code "for substantial and compelling reasons" (Section 14.15 (703)(3)).

The circumstances which may cause abuse of prescription drugs within the epidemiologic triangle are thus not specifically addressed in the state sentencing schemes. The circumstances of such abuse are not recognized by law.

Regulation of the Hosts in the Prescription of Controlled Substances: A Potential Administrative Morass

New York state has perhaps the most tightly controlled and elaborate system for the regulation of prescriptions for controlled substances under Schedules II, III, IV and V. As in all other states with prescription regulations, practitioners in New York can only make prescriptions in "good faith and in the course of professional practice." Similarly, a pharmacist can only dispense controlled substances while acting in "good faith and in the course of his professional practice" (Section 3333). Each controlled substance may be dispensed only if it is enclosed within a suitable and durable container, which has affixed to the container a label which is indelibly typed, printed, or otherwise written, including the name and address of the ultimate user and the name and address and phone number of the dispensing practitioner. In addition, New York requires a legend, prominently marked or printed in bold face or upper case lettering which states "controlled substance, dangerous unless used as directed." The container containing the substance must be identified with an orange label or label of another color which is superimposed on orange transparent adhesive tape (Title 44, New York Laws Annotated Section 3331 (1)).

New York requires each such prescription for Schedule II CDS and for benzodiazepines (Schedule IV CDS) to be written on an official New York State prescription form which must be prepared in triplicate, written with ink, indelible pencil, or typewriter. The prescriptions must be specific as to name, address, and age of ultimate user and must include the specific directions for use (New York Laws Annotated, Section 3332 *et. seq.*). The same mandate with respect to the container and labeling are required of the pharmacist who sells or dispenses the controlled substance to the ultimate user.

New York and New Jersey also allow the oral or telephone prescription of Schedule II drugs in a medical "emergency." "Emergency" is defined in New York State, for example, by the rules and/or regulations of the New York State Department of Health. A practitioner may orally prescribe, and a pharmacist dispense to an ultimate user, a controlled substance described in Schedule II provided that a pharmacist contemporaneously reduces the prescription to writing, dispenses the substance in conformity with the labelling requirements, and makes a good faith effort to verify the practitioner's identity if the practitioner is unknown to the pharmacist. The pharmacist cannot make a prescription which would exceed a five day supply if the substance were used in accordance with the directions for use.

Within seventy-two hours after authorizing an emergency oral prescription, the prescribing practitioner shall cause to be delivered to the pharmacist the original and one copy of an official New York State prescription form. In addition to the other information required on the form, this form must state "authorization for emergency dispensing" (Section 3334).

New York also requires that practitioners preserve the retained copy of the official New York State prescription form in a separate file maintained exclusively for such records (Section 33343).

Finally, the ultimate user of a controlled substance which was issued through a prescription must maintain the controlled substance in the original container in which it was dispensed. A violation of this provision is the subject of a separate criminal offense (Section 3345).

California has a similarly complex scheme of regulations. Responsibility for proper prescriptions, like New York, lies not only with the individual physician-practitioner but also with the pharmacist who fills the prescription (Section 11153(a) of the California code).

For example, prescription blanks must be issued by the California Department of Justice in serially numbered groups of not more than 100 forms each in triplicate and must be furnished to the practitioner authorized to write prescriptions for controlled substances classified in Schedule II. The prescription forms are not transferrable, and the Department of Justice may not issue more than 100 blanks during any 30 day period without written and approved justification. Possession of a blank prescription form other than as set forth in the California code is a misdemeanor (Section 11161(a)).

The possession of three or more counterfeit blank prescription forms is a crime punishable by not more than one year in prison (Section 11163(a)).

Like New York, California provides for the prescription of a Schedule II controlled substance in the event of an emergency. A practitioner may dispense directly to an ultimate user, a Schedule II controlled substance in an amount not to exceed a 72-hour supply pursuant to the practitioner's directions and only where the patient is not expected to require additional controlled substances beyond 72 hours.

Like New York, each prescription for a controlled substance in Schedule II must be written in ink or indelible pencil in the prescriber's handwriting on the approved Department of Justice form. As with prescriptions for other controlled substances on Schedule III, IV and V, the prescriptions must be in triplicate, signed by the prescriber with the name and address of the person for whom this controlled substance is prescribed, including the name, quantity, and strength of this controlled substance and directions for use. The dispensing pharmacy must retain a duplicate of the prescription forms. The original prescription form must be properly endorsed by the pharmacist with the name and address of the pharmacy and the pharmacy's state license number, the date the prescription was filled and the signature of the pharmacist. The original form must be transmitted to the Department of Justice at the end of each month in which the prescriptions were filled.

Perhaps the most stringent "emergency" prescription regulations for Schedule II substances are in force in Texas. Prescriptions made in an emergency situation must conform to Texas' triplicate prescription program (Section 481.075). The Texas triplicate program requires a practitioner who prescribes a controlled substance within Schedule II to record the prescription on an official form, in triplicate, and that the original copy be labeled "copy one" that the duplicate copy be labeled "copy two" and the triplicate copy be labeled "copy three." Each form must contain space in which to indicate the date the prescription was written, the date the prescription was filled, the drug prescribed, the dosage, the instructions for use, the name, address and Federal Drug Enforcement Administration (DEA) number of the dispensing pharmacy, the name of the pharmacist who filled the prescription, and the name, address and age of the person for whom the controlled substance is prescribed.

A substance listed in Schedule II, may be prescribed orally or by telephone communication by a practitioner. The individual dispensing the substance shall promptly write the oral or telephonically-communicated prescription and include the written record of the prescription, and other information listed above regarding dosage, instructions and identification of the ultimate user, to the Texas Department of Public Safety no later than thirty days after the prescription is filled. Texas also has a 72-hour rule which requires that after authorizing an emergency oral or telephonically-communicated prescription, the prescribing practitioner shall provide a written prescription, completed in the manner as required above, to be delivered *in person or mailed* to the dispensing pharmacist at the pharmacy where the prescription was dispensed. The envelope of a prescription mailed by mail must be postmarked not later than 72 hours after the prescription was authorized. On receipt of the prescription, the dispensing pharmacy must file the transcription of the telephonically-communicated prescription and the pharmacy copy.

Revocation and Suspension of License to Practice Medicine
Based on a Violation of a Prescription Regulation

The individual States have promulgated statutory provisions for the revocation and/or suspension of a medical practitioner's license on the basis that the practitioner prescribed drugs in a wrongful or excessive manner. Although revocation and/or suspension can occur within a wide variety of factual contexts, most instances arise when the practitioner prescribes a drug without medical justification or when the prescription is made in excessive amounts or dosages.

Without Medical Justification

Revocation has occurred in cases in which physicians prescribed drugs to undercover police agents without performing physical examinations and because refills of the prescription were honored simply by request of the patient (*Martinez vs. State Board of Medical Examiners,* 476 SW 2d 400 (1972)). Revocation has also occurred where a physician was prescribing Methaqualone for his fiancee and for another physician in order to obtain all or part of the drug for his personal use. The same physician also prescribed medication for individuals without first examining them or without establishing whether the drugs prescribed were medically indicated (*Quintana vs. Commonwealth State Board of Osteopathic Medical Examiners,* 466 A.2d 250 (1983)). The dispensing of weight control drugs, through prescription, but without medical necessity, has been sufficient to justify revocation of a physician's license to practice (*Pincus vs. Commonwealth State Board of Medical Education,* 424 A.2d 999 (1981)). License revocation was also appropriate where the physician wrote 521 prescriptions for Methaqualone during 527 alleged patient visits without medical justification, and kept insufficient records regarding the patients he treated, and failed to conduct a detailed drug use history or inquire into the cause of each patient's purported stress and insomnia (*Massey v. Ambach,* 522 NYS 2nd 989 (1987)). Since it is common that no one particular infraction is given as the sole reason for revocation, it is possible that even the least serious infraction (insufficient record keeping) can lead to revocation or suspension. State boards of examiners for the healing arts typically have wide discretion in discipline and punishment of their licenses.

For example, license revocation has occurred for issuance of only three prescriptions for sedative-hypnotics ("sleeping pills") to undercover narcotics investigators without a physical examination, and not given in good faith or in the regular course of practice (*Dannenberg v. Board of Regents,* 430 NYS 2nd 700 (1980)), compared with the mere suspension of a license to practice medicine because on two occasions the physician dispensed Phentermine and Phendimetrazine to patients who were under his continuing care for obesity control without first giving them physical examinations (*Scheininger vs. Department of Professional Regulation,* 443 SO 2nd 487 (1983)).

Excessive Dosage

A dental license suspension was upheld when evidence indicated that the prescription of heavy doses of Dilaudid as a pain reliever would promote further addiction to the drug (*Bowman vs. Texas State of Board of Dental Examiners*, 783 SW 2d 318 (1990)). Similarly, a physician's license was suspended for prescribing drugs to a former patient's widow following the death of her husband from cancer, upon his diagnosis of her condition as severe depression and possible renal colic and where it appeared that the widow was receiving approximately three times the dosage prescribed in an approved drug treatment program (*Pannone vs. New York State Educational Department*, 388 NYS 2d 174 (1976)). In a contrary case, a physician's license was not affected for prescribing controlled substances to four patients where all four patients had serious medical problems and suffered chronic and severe pain for which Dilaudid provided the only substantial relief. The evidence further showed that the physician acted reasonably in his treatment of the patients and the prescription for each patient did not exceed the recommended dosage in that at least some of the patients were possibly already habituated or tolerant to that drug at the time it was prescribed (*Johnston vs. Department of Professional Regulation*, 454 SO 2nd 795 (1984)).

Suspension and/or revocation can take place for various other reasons including failure to keep complete and accurate records of purchases and disposal of controlled drugs (for example, in one situation where a physician purchased 148,700 dosage units of Methaqualane at 300 mg each but could only account for 14,242 dispensed doses (*Lepere vs. Texas State Board of Medical Examiners*, 654 SW 2d 796 (1983)). A physician who signed prescription pads in blank was placed on probation for two years, although the purpose of the preassigned prescription was to allow a nurse-midwife to order a prenatal and postnatal vitamin/mineral/iron preparation for patients. In this case, attempt was made to provide controlled substances for the physician, nurse, or patients (*Boggs vs. State Board of Medical Examiners*, 341 SE 2.d 635 (1986)).

Other reasons for suspension and revocation in the prescription drug context occur when licensees unlawfully dispense drugs to known drug addicts or when they permit unauthorized persons to prescribe drugs (*Shakin v. Board of Medical Examiners*, 254 Cal App 2d 102 (1967), and *Arkansas State Medical Board vs. Grimmett*, 463 SW 2d 662 (1971)).

Procedural Mechanisms for Revocation
of Medical and Dental Licenses

The administrative procedures for the revocation and/or suspension of a license to practice medicine, pharmacy, or dentistry are initiated by the various state licensing boards. Typically, a licensing board can initiate a revocation proceeding if a practitioner has been convicted of a crime involving moral turpitude ("turpitude" is broadly construed to include almost any type of criminal conduct), or when there has been a violation of a any provision for the administration of prescription of drugs. Revocation occurs only after a hearing, unless the practitioner admits to the charge and submits to a sentencing proceeding. The licensing boards only require that the charges be sustained by a "preponderance of the evidence." This level of proof merely requires that the finder of fact conclude that the evidence show that it is "more likely than not" that the alleged violation occurred (*See N.J.S.A.,* 49:9–16).

CONCLUSION

Within the epidemiologic triangle model, the legislative bodies which govern the lawful use and punishment for unlawful use of prescription drugs have made the hosts the focus of their legislative efforts. Indeed, the sheer mass of statutory and administrative regulation falls disproportionately on the conduct of the hosts. While we do not ascribe to the view that more is necessarily better, it appears that little legislative attention is paid/made to the environment. Since the abuse and dependence in prescription drugs carries with it unique imitation and recurrence characteristics, it would make sound policy to direct legislative efforts to meet those particular characteristics of prescription drug abuse and dependence so as to institute preventive measures/rehabilitated measures in the context of the criminal sentence/legal disposition of offenders.

Endnote

[1]*See* Sections 204, 206, 208, 210 and 212 of Uniform Laws Annotated, Volume 9, Part 2, 1992.

REFERENCES

Arkansas State Medical Board v. Grimmett, 463 S.W. 2d 662 (1971).

Boggs v. State Board of Medical Examiners, 341 S.E. 2d 635 (1986).

Bowman v. Texas State Board of Dental Examiners, 783 S.W. 2d 318 (1990).

California Code Annotated, Section 11153(1).

Dannenberg v. Board of Regents, 430 N.Y.S. 2d. 700 (1980).

Johnston v. Department of Professional Regulation, 454 So. 2d 795 (1984).

Lepere v. Texas State Board of Medical Examiners, 654 S.W. 2d 796 (1983).

Martinez v. State Board of Medical Examiners, 476 S.W. 2d 400 (1972).

Massey v. Ambagh, 522 N.Y.S. 2d 989 (1987).

Michigan Laws Annotated, 14.15(703)(3).

New Jersey Statutes Annotated 2C:44-1 et. seq.

New Jersey Statutes Annotated 49:9–16.

New York Laws Annotated, Title 44, Section 3311(1).

New York Laws Annotated, Title 44, Section 3333.

Pannone v. New York State Educational Department, 388 N.Y.S. 2d. 174(1976).

Pincus v. Commonwealth State Board of Medical Education, 424 A. 2d 999 (1981).Quintana v. Commonwealth State Board of Osteopathic Medical Examiners, 466 A. 2d 250 (1983).

Scheininger v. Department of Professional Regulation, 443 So. 2d 487 (1983).

Shakin v. Board of Medical Examiners, 254 Cal. App. 2d 102 (1967).

Texas Code Annotated, Section 481.075.

Chapter 10

IN CONCLUSION: AN EPILOGUE

DANIEL P. GREENFIELD

"That physicians could be considered the gatekeepers to Paradise is unsettling" (Weiss and Greenfield, 1986). Conversely, " . . . the Biblical phrase, 'There but for the grace of God go I' applies to all of us who use these drugs" (Russo, this volume). In the context of these two seemingly disparate statements, prescription drug abuse and dependence (PDAD) presents an interesting and complex meeting of two very different sets of participants—the prescribers and their consumers. From the prescriber's perspective, legal regulation and constraint—although often unwelcome in a prescriber's professional practice—can provide a reason *not* to prescribe a perhaps necessary medication, generally a psychoactive one. On the other hand, from the perspective of a potential consumer of prescriber's services, those services as a source of high-quality drugs can be very appealing, even though the legal risks are similar to other legal risks of other types of drug-seeking behaviors. In both cases, PDAD has been present for many years, and is likely to continue to be, even if it constitutes only a small part of total drug abuse and dependence.

In this monograph, we have presented information and material which will be useful to prescribers and other health care professionals who treat and work with drug abusing and dependent client/patients, including PDAD client/patients. By being aware of the existence and extent of this problem; by being knowledgeable about all three elements ("host," "agent," and "environment") of the "epidemiologic triangle" model of PDAD; and by being aware of services, help, and treatment available—when applicable—to patients and prescribers alike, those health-care providers and their nonprescriber colleagues will be in better position to help both their patients and themselves.

We hope and believe that this monograph will be useful to all involved in all three elements of the PDAD epidemiologic triangle — to prescribers and their colleagues, and to patients.

REFERENCES

Russo, R. (1994). Foreword. *Prescription Drug Abuse and Dependence.* (Page ix) Springfield: Charles C Thomas Publisher.
Weiss, K. and Greenfield, D. (1986). Prescription Drug Abuse. *Psychiatric Clinics of No. Amer., 9:* 475–490.

AUTHOR INDEX

153

SUBJECT INDEX